CAMBRIDGE LIBRARY COLLECTION

Books of enduring scholarly value

Music

The systematic academic study of music gave rise to works of description, analysis and criticism, by composers and performers, philosophers and anthropologists, historians and teachers, and by a new kind of scholar - the musicologist. This series makes available a range of significant works encompassing all aspects of the developing discipline.

A Treatise on Harmony

Sir Frederick Arthur Gore Ouseley (1825–1889), English church musician, composer, Professor of Music at Oxford and Precentor of Hereford Cathedral, is best remembered for the foundation of St Michael's College, Tenbury, and its extensive music library in 1856. Here he was concerned to maintain the tradition of sung daily offices and to provide a model for others to follow. This book, first published in 1868, is the first of Ouseley's three works on music theory, and offers a structured approach to the subject, beginning with an explanation of musical notation and the harmonic series, then moving through the rules of harmony from tonic and dominant triads, to chord inversions, augmentation, diminution, modulation, the use of suspensions, pivot notes and cadence sequences. Of interest to music students and historians, the book contains exercises for the student and an appendix giving a number of musical examples.

Cambridge University Press has long been a pioneer in the reissuing of out-of-print titles from its own backlist, producing digital reprints of books that are still sought after by scholars and students but could not be reprinted economically using traditional technology. The Cambridge Library Collection extends this activity to a wider range of books which are still of importance to researchers and professionals, either for the source material they contain, or as landmarks in the history of their academic discipline.

Drawing from the world-renowned collections in the Cambridge University Library, and guided by the advice of experts in each subject area, Cambridge University Press is using state-of-the-art scanning machines in its own Printing House to capture the content of each book selected for inclusion. The files are processed to give a consistently clear, crisp image, and the books finished to the high quality standard for which the Press is recognised around the world. The latest print-on-demand technology ensures that the books will remain available indefinitely, and that orders for single or multiple copies can quickly be supplied.

The Cambridge Library Collection will bring back to life books of enduring scholarly value (including out-of-copyright works originally issued by other publishers) across a wide range of disciplines in the humanities and social sciences and in science and technology.

A Treatise on Harmony

FREDERICK ARTHUR GORE OUSELEY

CAMBRIDGE
UNIVERSITY PRESS

CAMBRIDGE UNIVERSITY PRESS

Cambridge, New York, Melbourne, Madrid, Cape Town,
Singapore, São Paolo, Delhi, Tokyo, Mexico City

Published in the United States of America by Cambridge University Press, New York

www.cambridge.org
Information on this title: www.cambridge.org/9781108030229

© in this compilation Cambridge University Press 2011

This edition first published 1868
This digitally printed version 2011

ISBN 978-1-108-03022-9 Paperback

Clarendon Press Series

PRINCIPLES OF HARMONY

OUSELEY

London

MACMILLAN AND CO.

𝕮𝖑𝖆𝖗𝖊𝖓𝖉𝖔𝖓 𝕻𝖗𝖊𝖘𝖘 𝕾𝖊𝖗𝖎𝖊𝖘

A

TREATISE ON HARMONY

BY THE

REV. SIR F. A. GORE OUSELEY, BART., M.A., MUS. DOC.

PROFESSOR OF MUSIC IN THE UNIVERSITY OF OXFORD

𝕺𝖝𝖋𝖔𝖗𝖉

AT THE CLARENDON PRESS

M.DCCC.LXVIII

PREFACE.

THE object aimed at in this volume is the combination of true philosophical principles with simplicity of explanation. It also endeavours to include all necessary details in the smallest possible compass.

So many treatises on Harmony have appeared since the beginning of this century, that some apology is perhaps due for adding yet one more to the number. The author must plead as his apology, the conviction that although the existing treatises on the subject contain much very valuable matter, yet all seem to him to be either founded on erroneous principles, or faulty in arrangement. Some mix up together the elements of Harmony, Counterpoint, and Pianoforte-practice; others start from principles not based upon nature, but too often contradicted by the now better ascertained phenomena of acoustics; others repudiate physical science altogether, and treat of Music as though it were only an emotional art. The present volume tries to avoid these and other similar errors.

Wherever existing works explain or illustrate any point with clearness, they have been quoted freely and acknowledged with gratitude. But in other and more frequent cases it has been necessary to take up entirely fresh ground, and to employ new explanations and illustrations. It is confidently hoped that the system thus evolved may prove useful to the student, by giving him natural and rational explanations of the facts of Music, and of the rules deduced from those facts. The author has aimed throughout at a consistent theory, founded in nature, progressively expanded, and involving no purely arbitrary rules. He now lays the results of his endeavours before the public.

His warmest thanks are due to many who have aided him in the production of this work, especially to Professor Pole, Mus. Doc., for his admirable illustration of the comparative magnitude of intervals, and the lucid explanations accompanying it, which invest the work with a scientific value it would not otherwise have possessed.

In conclusion, a suggestion is offered as to the best way of using this little work. The student is recommended to study Harmony and Counterpoint *concurrently*, working at them a little at a time, alternately. He will find that neither can be perfectly mastered without the other. With this view, the author proposes, before long, to bring out a Treatise on Counterpoint, based on those of Fux, Marpurg, Reicha, and Cherubini, which will be so constructed as to run parallel to the present volume, as far as possible; and he desires that the two works may be regarded as parts of one whole, for the instruction of such as desire to grasp the subject in its completeness.

St. Michael's College, Tenbury,
January, 1868.

OUSELEY'S HARMONY.

Instructions to binder.

Table of Intervals to precede page 1, mount by right edge.
Plate I to face page 262. Plate II to face page 263.
Backing one another.

TABLE OF CONTENTS.

b

CHAPTER XI.

CHAPTER XII.

CHAPTER XIII.

CHAPTER XIV.

CHAPTER XV.

CHAPTER XVI.

CHAPTER XVII.

CHAPTER XVIII.

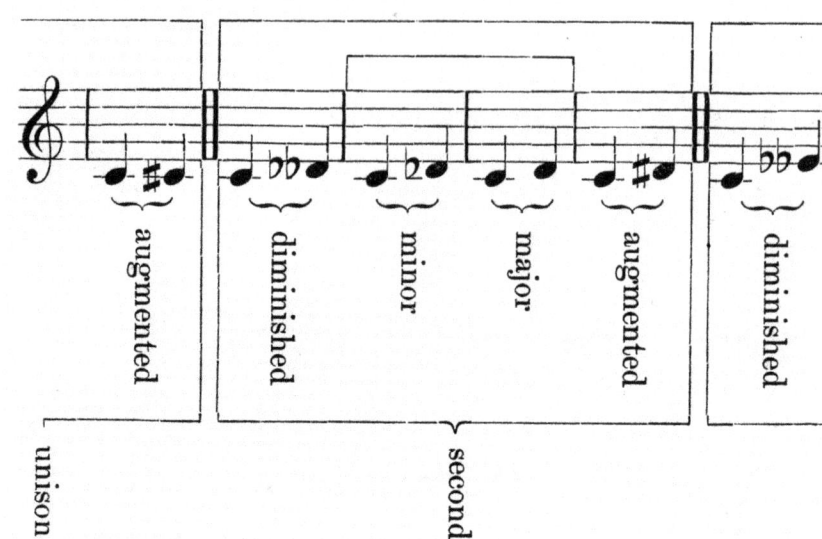

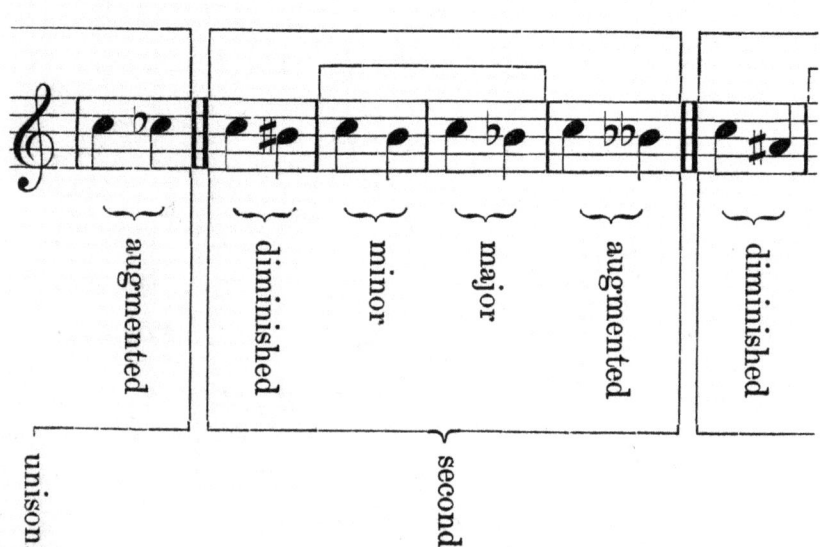

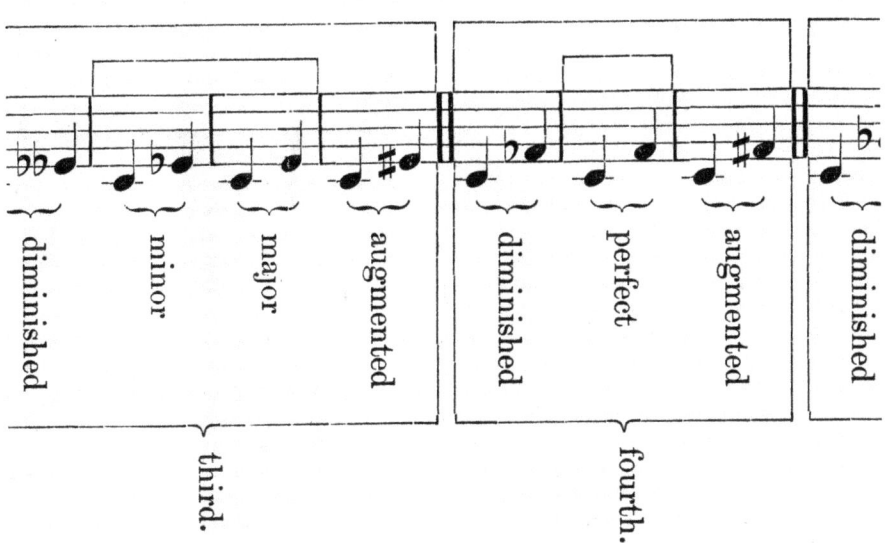

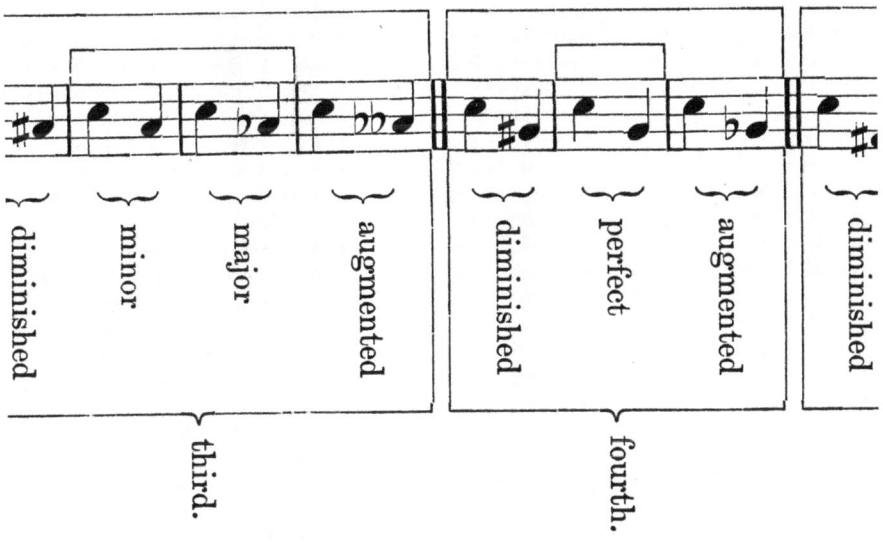

This nomenclature will be strictly adhe

INTERVALS.

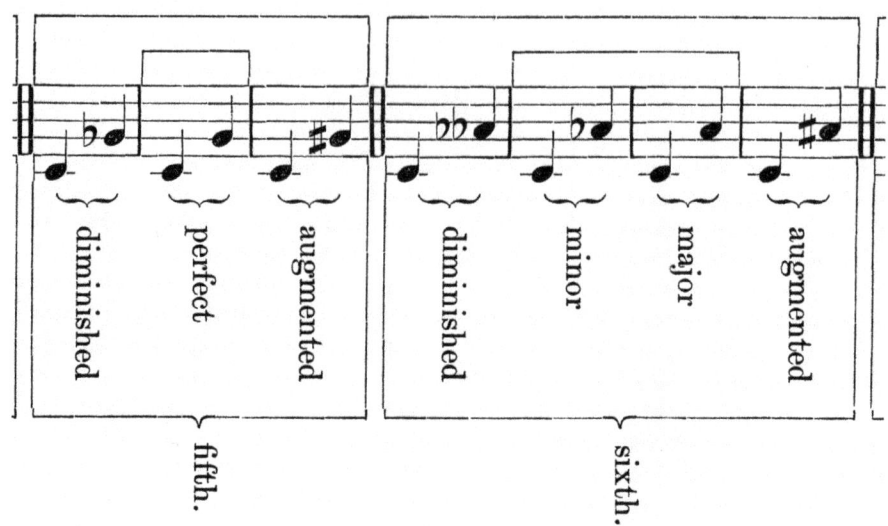

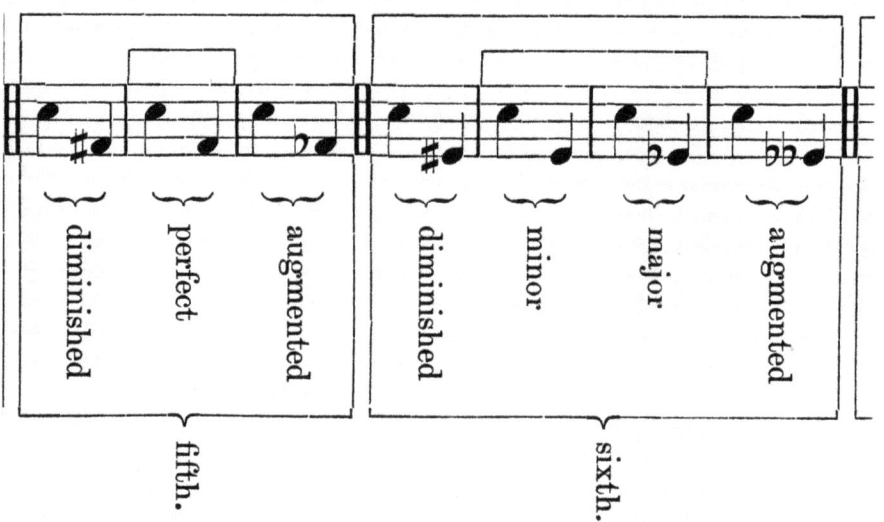

adhered to throughout this treatise.

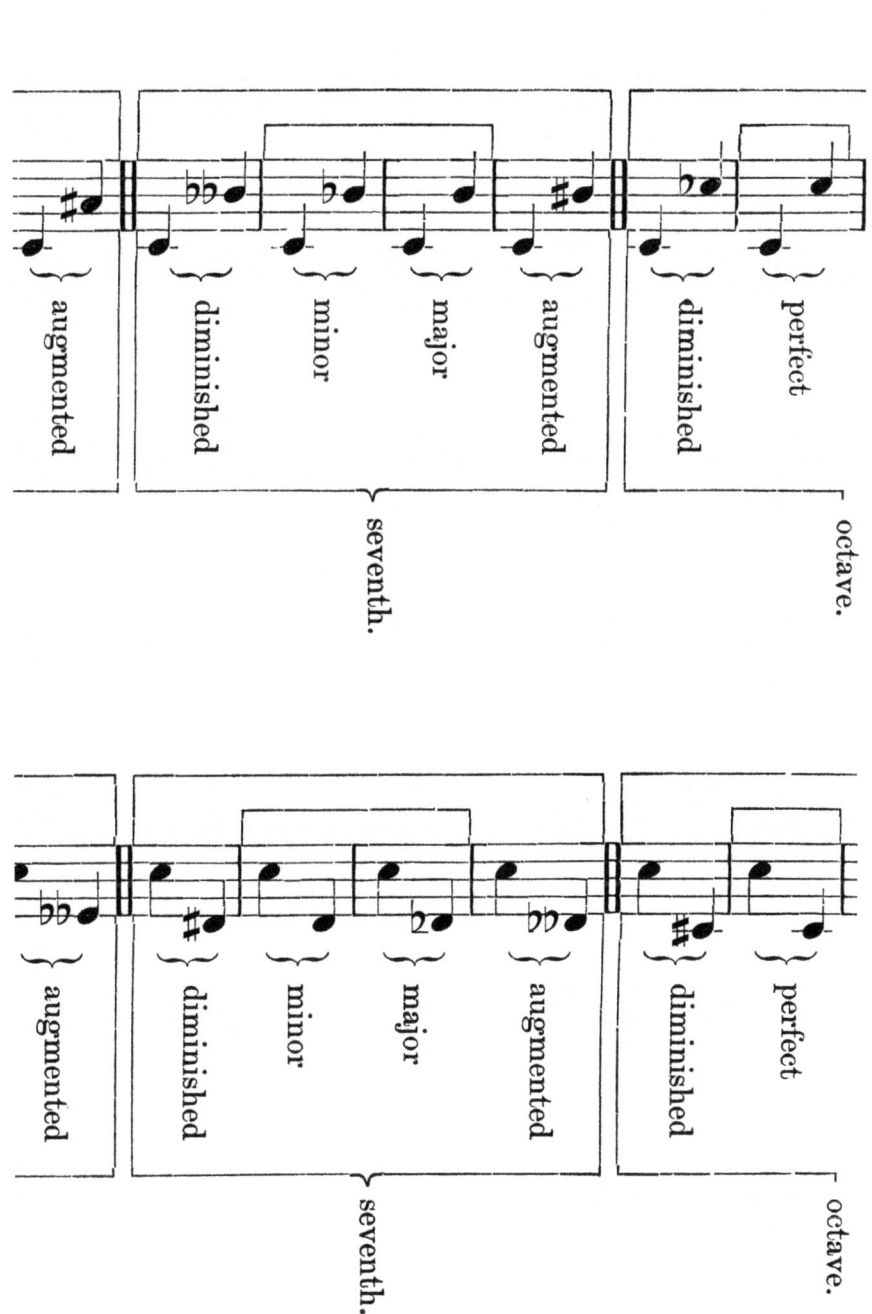

A SHORT TREATISE

ON THE

PRINCIPLES OF HARMONY.

CHAPTER I.

Preliminary Remarks.

1. IT is presumed that the student who uses this book is already acquainted with what are commonly considered the first elements of music. A very brief summary of these will, therefore, be all that is required here, before we begin to treat of harmony strictly so called. And it will be sufficient for our purpose to indicate most of these elementary matters in a tabular form, as our chief object in so doing is merely to set forth the system of nomenclature which will be adhered to in these pages.

2. In the first place, it is important that the student should have clear views as to musical notation. For this purpose he is referred to Hullah's admirable little Treatise on the Stave, than which nothing can be more definite and intelligible.

He will there learn, that our ordinary stave of five lines is derived from what is called *the great stave of eleven*—

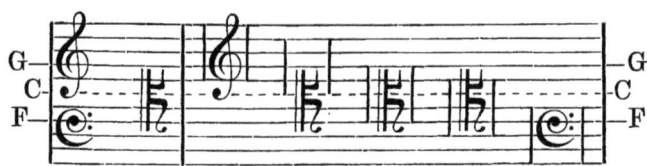

The three lines to which the letters G, C, and F are here appended, represent fixed sounds of definite pitch : from these all others are counted. Formerly, the whole eleven lines were occasionally used, and sometimes six, seven, four, or three. But five lines have been found sufficient for all purposes, and that number is now universally employed.

It is obvious that in selecting the five adjacent lines which we shall use for our stave, we must be guided by a consideration of the notes we have to write, and their place in the scale or range of musical sounds.

If we are writing for violins, flutes, or other high-toned instruments, or for treble voices, or for the upper portion of keyed instruments, it will be necessary to select the topmost lines of the great stave. These five lines do not include either the fixed note C or the fixed note F, but they do include the fixed note G, which is represented by the figure called the G clef—or treble clef—or violin clef, and which will be placed so that the principal curl of it shall fall on the second line counting upwards; thus .

If we are writing for bass instruments or voices, it will be necessary to select the five lines at the bottom of the great stave. These will not include either the fixed notes G or C, but only the fixed note F, which is represented by the figure ⊃: or ℰ:, called the bass clef, and which will be placed so that the two dots shall fall above and below the fourth line counting upwards; thus F——.

Instruments of large range, such as the organ, pianoforte, or harp,

require the combination of these two staves; thus

and on comparing this with the great stave, it will be seen that it contains the whole of it except the middle line, which represents the fixed note C.

If we are writing for instruments of medium range, such as the viola, or the alto and tenor trombones, or for contralto or tenor voices, neither of the above staves will be found convenient; the one being too high and the other too low in the scale: therefore we must select some other set of five lines, to suit the requirements of the case. Whichever set we select will include always two and sometimes the three fixed notes in the great stave; and as we have already appropriated the clefs representing G and F to the highest and lowest staves respectively, it will conduce to clearness and distinction if we use the symbol of the fixed note C, which is thus formed, ᛄ, or ᛃ, to distinguish our medium staves.

Of such staves only three are now in use.

The most acute is called the soprano, and is used in instrumental scores of oratorios, and in old Church music, for the soprano or treble voices. It consists of the 6th, 7th, 8th, 9th, and 10th lines of the great stave, counting upwards, and is expressed thus C———G.

The next is the truly medium stave, and consists of the 4th, 5th, 6th, 7th, and 8th lines of the great stave, counting upwards. It is used for the viola, or alto violin, for the alto trombone, and for the alto voice parts in scores. It is expressed thus C.

The last is called the tenor clef (or, more properly, the tenor *stave*), and is used for the tenor voices in scores, as well as for the tenor trombone, and sometimes also for the higher notes of the violoncello and bassoon. It consists of the 3rd, 4th, 5th, 6th, and 7th lines of the great stave, counting upwards, and is expressed thus C.

For further details the student is referred to Hullah's book above-mentioned, or to Marx's "Theory and Practice of Musical Composition," (translated by Saroni. New York, 1852).

3. It will be sufficient to give a list of the different kinds of notes and rests, an ordinary acquaintance with them being presupposed.

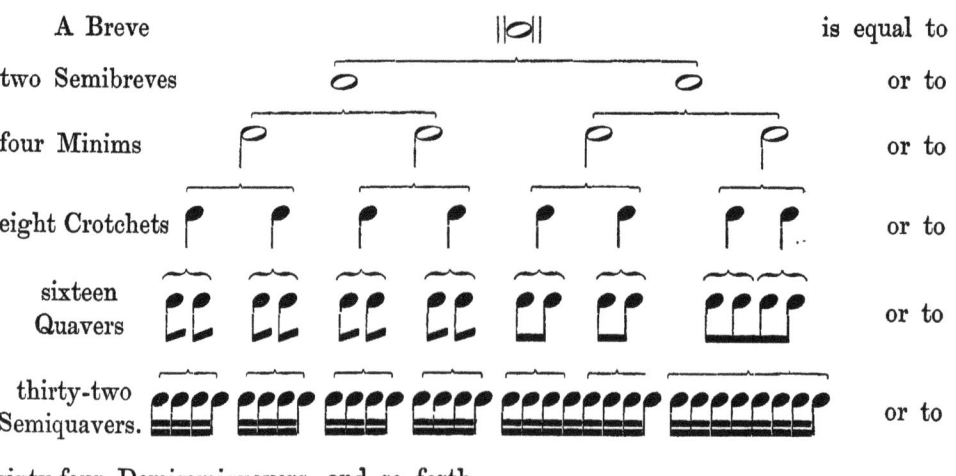

A Breve		is equal to
two Semibreves		or to
four Minims		or to
eight Crotchets		or to
sixteen Quavers		or to
thirty-two Semiquavers.		or to

sixty-four Demisemiquavers, and so forth.

The corresponding *rests* (to represent intervals of silence) are the breve ▦, the semibreve ▦, the minim ▦, the crotchet ⸀, the quaver ⸀, the semiquaver ⸀, and the demisemiquaver ⸀.

A dot after a note or rest makes it half as long again: thus ○·, or a dotted semibreve, is equivalent to three minims, or six crotchets, or twelve quavers: ⸀·, or a dotted minim, is equivalent to three crotchets, or six quavers, or twelve semiquavers.

If a second dot is added, it will lengthen the note or rest half as much again as the first dot: thus ⸀··, or a doubly dotted crotchet, is equivalent to seven semiquavers, or fourteen demisemiquavers; for it consists of the value of a crotchet, a quaver, and a semiquaver, i. e. two quavers, one quaver, and a semiquaver, i. e. four semiquavers, two semiquavers, and one semiquaver, i. e. $4 + 2 + 1 = 7$ semiquavers.

When a note or a rest is to be lengthened *indefinitely*, this figure ⌢, called a *pause*, is placed under or over it.

For further details and exercises on this branch of musical knowledge we must refer to more elementary treatises.

4. Supposing the student to be familiar with the use of bars and double bars, with the theory of accent, and the art of beating time, it will be sufficient for our purpose to give a time-table, to shew the system and arrangement adopted in this book.

a. Common or Duple Time—divided into

i. Simple, and ii. Compound.

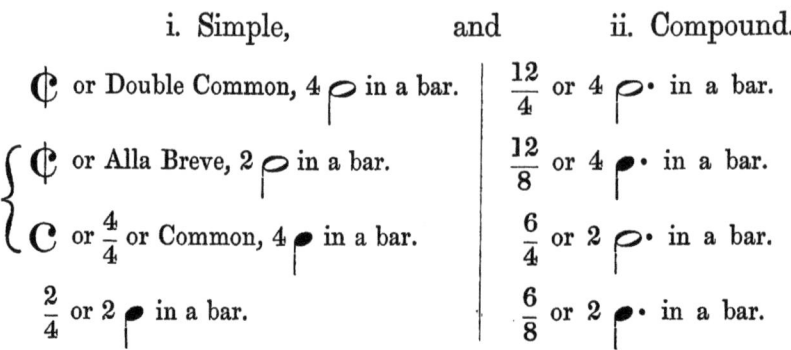

β. Triple Time—divided into

i. Simple, and ii. Compound.

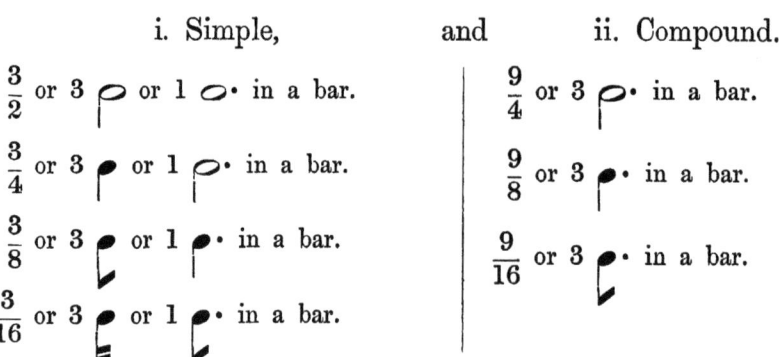

5. It may be taken for granted that the student knows the meanings of the figures ♯, ♭, ♮, ×, ♭♭, and the use of them, both as *accidentals* and in the *signature*. If not, we must again refer him back to the elementary treatises, contenting ourselves with a tabular list of the keys, major and minor, with their several signatures.

Major keys with sharps.		Minor keys with sharps.	
7 sharps	C♯	7 sharps	A♯
6 sharps	F♯	6 sharps	D♯
5 sharps	B♮	5 sharps	G♯
4 sharps	E♮	4 sharps	C♯
3 sharps	A♮	3 sharps	F♯
2 sharps	D♮	2 sharps	B♮
1 sharp	G♮	1 sharp	E♮

Major natural key . .	C♮	Minor natural key . .	A♮

Major keys with flats.		Minor keys with flats.	
1 flat	F♮	1 flat	D♮
2 flats	B♭	2 flats	G♮
3 flats	E♭	3 flats	C♮
4 flats	A♭	4 flats	F♮
5 flats	D♭	5 flats	B♭
6 flats	G♭	6 flats	E♭
7 flats	C♭	7 flats	A♭

Each of these major keys is supposed to be *nearly related* to that minor key which has the same signature, and stands on a line with it in the above table : hence the terms *relative major* and *relative minor*.

6. It will be necessary to give a table of intervals, although it is supposed that the student has already mastered them before using this book, because some of them have been variously named by different writers, and it is essential, as a preliminary, to fix our own nomenclature, which will be strictly adhered to in the following pages.

Intervals are divided into *consonant* and *dissonant* intervals, (or, as they are sometimes called, *concords* and *discords*).

Consonant intervals are of two kinds, *perfect* and *imperfect*.

Imperfect consonant intervals are subdivided again into *major* and *minor*.

Perfect consonances cannot be so subdivided.

Dissonant intervals also, like the imperfect consonances, are either *major* or *minor*.

All intervals are susceptible likewise of certain *alterations*, called augmentation and diminution ; excepting only that *major* intervals cannot be *diminished*, and that *minor* intervals cannot be *augmented*.

Perfect consonances alone can both be diminished and augmented.

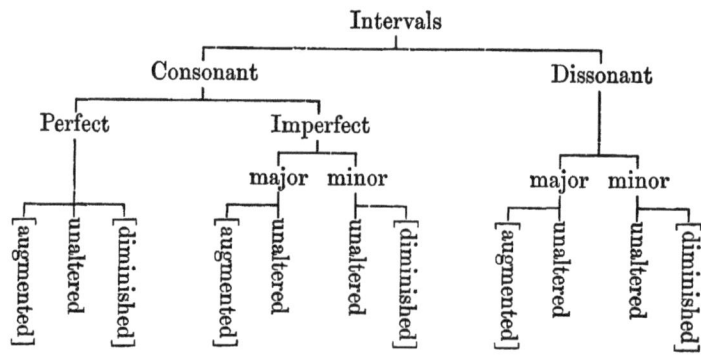

The smallest unaltered interval is the minor second, or semitone : and it is convenient to compare and measure all larger intervals by the number of semitones they contain, or to which they are equivalent.

The perfect consonant intervals, according to the usual computation, are the octave and the fifth; to which may be added the fourth also, though only under certain restrictions, to be considered hereafter.

The imperfect consonant intervals are the major and minor third, and the major and minor sixth.

The dissonant intervals are the second and the seventh, each of which may also be major or minor.

If the interval of a semitone be subtracted from any perfect or minor interval, by means of a sharp or flat, to *alter* the pitch of the lower or upper notes respectively, such interval is said to be diminished.

If by the same means a perfect or major interval be enlarged to the same extent, such interval is said to be augmented.

All augmented or diminished intervals so produced are called *chromatic dissonances*, except the two which occur in the diatonic major scale, i. e. the *augmented fourth* or *tritone* between the 4th and 7th degree, and the *diminished fifth* between the 7th degree and the 4th in the next octave. Of all which more will be said hereafter.

If an octave be added to any interval, its original character (as regards divisibility into major, minor, augmented, or diminished) remains the same; only that in the case of the 2nd, 3rd, 4th, 5th, and 6th, they are in that case sometimes designated as the 9th, 10th, 11th, 12th, 13th, as will be more fully explained in a future section.

We here annex a list of all the intervals, illustrated in the key of C natural.

NOTE. Some writers call augmented intervals "extreme." Others call augmented perfect intervals "pluperfect." Others call diminished fifths "false fifths." Others call augmented fourths "tritones." Others call minor sevenths and seconds " flat." Others call major sevenths and seconds "sharp." Others call diminished fourths "flattened." Others call augmented fifths "sharp."

But every one of these terms is unsystematic and unphilosophical, and some of them are absolutely incorrect.

7. There are yet remaining a few technical terms which ought to be explained in this preliminary chapter.

(α) A *chord* is the simultaneous sounding of several different notes, selected according to certain fixed principles and rules.

(β) A *triad* is a chord of three notes consisting of a bass with its

third and fifth, e. g.

Triads are of three kinds :—

　　　i. *Major;*　　　ii. *Minor;*　　　iii. *Imperfect,* or *diminished.*

A major triad consists of a major third and perfect fifth.

A minor triad consists of a minor third and perfect fifth.

An imperfect triad consists of a minor third and diminished fifth.

(γ) If the octave of the bass is added above a major or minor triad, it constitutes what is called a *common chord.*

NOTE. The imperfect triad being (as its name imports) *not* formed after the same perfect model as the major and minor triads, cannot be converted into a common chord by the addition of the octave of its lowest note.

(*Examples*)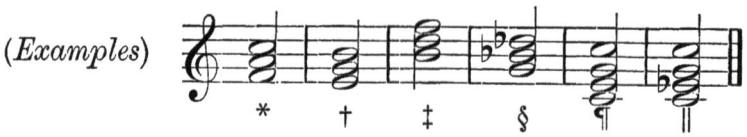

* A major triad.	† A minor triad.	‡ Imperfect triad.
§ Imperfect triad.	¶ Common chord major.	‖ Common chord minor.

Besides these triads we occasionally meet with what is called an augmented triad, which consists of a major third and augmented fifth, or of two major thirds superposed; thus  .

8. It may be as well here to explain one or two terms which belong rather to *counterpoint* than to *harmony*, but to which reference must necessarily be made in treating of the resolution of discords, and in some other cases also.

i. Motion is of three kinds :—similar, oblique, and contrary.

α. Similar motion is said to exist between any two or more parts, or voices, which ascend or descend simultaneously, but not in

unison; e. g.  &c.

β. Oblique motion is when one part remains without moving while another ascends or descends; e. g.

γ. Contrary motion is when two parts, or voices, move in opposite directions; e. g.

ii. Consecutive fifths or octaves are produced when two parts move so as to produce the same interval (of a fifth or an octave, as the

case may be) between them in successive chords.   There are several kinds of such consecutive fifths and octaves.

α. By similar motion ; e. g.

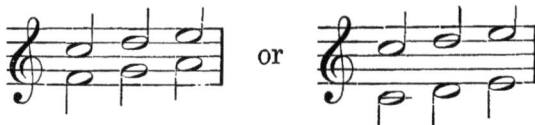

β. By contrary motion ; e. g.

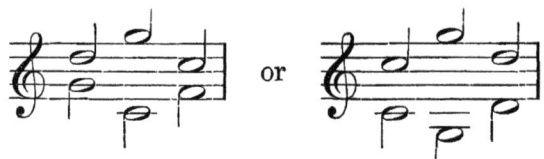

γ. Hidden fifths or octaves, which occur when an unaccented note intervenes without any change of fundamental harmony ; e. g.

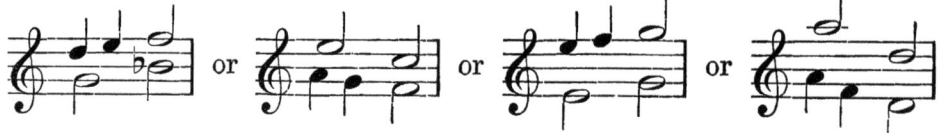

By the laws of strict counterpoint, every consecutive fifth or octave, of any of the above kinds, is altogether forbidden.

Consecutive major thirds have been likewise forbidden by some ancient authorities, though modern composers use them very freely.   Still it must be admitted that several unaccompanied major thirds in succession do produce a very disagreeable effect.   Any one playing the following notes on a keyed instrument will perceive their badness :—

Consecutive fourths are also strictly forbidden, unless accompanied by thirds below them, when they become perfectly correct and pleasant

to the ear ; thus is bad, while is good.

It is unnecessary to go any further now into this matter, as the harmonic principle involved will be duly explained in its proper place.

CHAPTER II.

First Principles of Harmony.

1. THE origin of harmony must be sought in natural phænomena. This involves an acquaintance with the science of acoustics, and is therefore more or less foreign to the peculiar subject of this treatise. Still, it will be necessary to observe here that the primary chord given us by nature is the following :—root, octave, twelfth, fifteenth, seventeenth, and nineteenth.

As an example of such a natural and primary chord, we will assume C as our root, or generator, and give the notes which result from it as natural harmonics :—

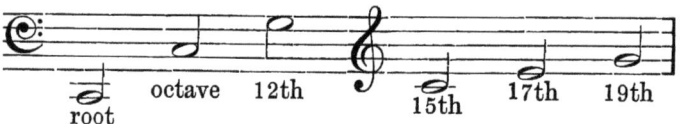

The interval of an octave is so perfect a concord, that it may be regarded as almost equivalent to an unison. It is therefore possible for us to omit for the present the root and its octave , as they are sufficiently represented by its double octave (or fifteenth), .

Similarly, we may for the present omit the twelfth of the root, , as it is sufficiently represented by its own octave , which is the nineteenth, or octave-twelfth, or double-octave-fifth, of the original generator.

We get then, as our residuum, the major triad , which is the primary harmony of nature.

2. If we were to continue the natural series of harmonic sounds as they occur in nature, we should arrive at some which would lead us out of the key in which we began, and which in fact do not belong to that key at all, but to others related to it in a peculiar way, which will be explained when we come to speak of *modulation*.

For instance, starting from the generator C, as before, we should find the following sequence of notes succeeding those given above :—

Now of these there are four, marked ×, which not only are foreign to the key of C, but are *out of tune* in any key.

Four others, marked ⊙, are merely repetitions of the intervals of the major triad in an upper octave. They may therefore be considered as identical with the primary chord we have already obtained.

Two only remain, D and B, which we can make use of for our present purpose.

On carefully examining these two notes, and combining them with the note *G* which we already possess, we find that they constitute together a major triad.

To shew this more clearly, let us take the highest G in the above figure,  :

the B next above it,  : and let us take the higher octave of the D, which is

written beyond the double bar, : and this gives us the major triad , of which G may be regarded as the generator, just as C is the generator of the triad

.

3. Seeing that octaves may be neglected in these considerations, it will be convenient to write this new major triad an octave lower, thus   ; and setting out the whole harmonic series of G, of which it forms the principal part, we produce this scheme—

No. i.   ii.   iii.   iv.   v.   vi.   vii.   viii.   ix.   x.   xi.   xii.   xiii.   xiv.   xv.   xvi.

Here it will be observed, that every note belongs to the key of C till we come to the double bar : and although the note F, marked ×, is not perfectly in tune, yet we can substitute a really true F without at all materially disturbing our new series of sounds.

Omitting, then, numbers i, ii, iii, viii, x, (and of course all beyond the double bar,) as we did in the case of the harmonic series of the generator C, we get as our residuum the chord , which is called the "dominant chord of nature," being based on the fifth of the key; which fifth is called *the dominant,* because it exercises the most powerful influence on the harmony.

Reducing our two chords to the same octave, and writing them in juxtaposition, , our ear at once detects a close relationship between them, and on hearing the former of the two, it immediately feels a desire to hear the latter also, and feels relieved and satisfied when it has been sounded.

4. From the preceding section it will have been seen that while the dominant harmony suggests the idea of *change* or *motion,* and tends to the primary major triad, that primary major triad suggests no such idea, but rather induces *rest,* and in fact determines the key in which the music is written ; gives, as it were, the characteristic *tone* to the music : hence

the original generator is called the *Tonic*, and its triad or common chord is called *Tonic harmony*.

If we were to be confined to tonic harmony alone, we should be like a prisoner within the four walls of a gaol—we could never get out of one groove. Our fatigue would become unbearable.

If this passage be played over several times, it will give a fair idea of the irksomeness of purely tonic harmony.

On the other hand, if we were confined to dominant harmony, not only should we have a continually unsatisfied craving after a Tonic chord, but we should be even more wearied than in the above case. An example will sufficiently prove this :—

Play over this exclusively dominant piece, and it will remind you of a traveller wandering homeless from place to place, seeking a welcome, and finding none.

But an alternation of tonic and dominant chords will always excite and satisfy the ear, just as alternate activity and rest are salutary and pleasant to the body.

5. It may, then, be taken as proved, that the key-note or tonic, with its third and fifth, satisfies the ear, and leads it to desire no further change. For this reason, the close or "perfect cadence" of a piece of music must always terminate in a tonic chord.

It may also be taken as proved, that the fifth of the tonic, which is called the dominant, with its third, fifth, minor seventh, and major ninth, does not satisfy the ear, but leads it to desire a change to the tonic harmony. For this reason the dominant harmony never can end a piece, but should *precede the tonic*.

And it is from this characteristic feature of the dominant harmony that the whole system of the resolution of fundamental discords is derived, of which we shall soon have to speak.

This is a most important first principle, and should be thoroughly understood and mastered by the pupil before going any further. For which object it is desirable that he should strike the following dominant chords, pausing after each, and realizing the unsatisfactory impression they leave on the ear :—

To shew how the ear may be satisfied by a tonic chord succeeding each of these dominant chords, let the student play the following :—

and he will perceive that in each case the tonic chord, which here succeeds the dominant, at once satisfies the ear, and produces the sensation of rest.

6. It must next be observed, that it is not *every* note in the dominant harmony which necessarily possesses the peculiarity of leading thus to the tonic. For if we simply take the major triad of the dominant root, there is nothing in it to shew that it is not a tonic triad : for instance, ♪ *may* be simply the tonic harmony of the key of G.

But the moment we add the next note in order which belongs to the dominant harmony, which in this case would be F, thus ♪ ,

we preclude all impressions of the key of G, or of G as a *tonic* root, for the F here is *natural*, and therefore out of the scale of G, which of course requires the F to be sharpened.

Moreover, the interval of a minor seventh, from G to F, and of a diminished fifth, from B to F, at once destroy all the *rest* and *permanence* of the chord.

This minor seventh, then, is clearly the characteristic note which invests the chord with its distinctively dominant character. Hence this chord is generally called the " chord of the dominant seventh."

NOTE. This chord is often called the " added seventh," because it is composed of a seventh added to a major triad. It is also sometimes called the " fundamental seventh," to distinguish it from other chords of the seventh. Likewise some writers call it the " minor seventh" chord. None of these designations are incorrect, but in this work it will be invariably styled the " chord of the dominant seventh."

7. This chord, as we have just seen, contains discords, and these are made to satisfy the ear by means of the chord of the tonic, which must follow immediately. When the discords have thus been rendered agreeable to the ear, they are said to be *resolved;* and this resolution of discords forms the most important element of the science of harmony.

The rule for resolving the chord of the dominant seventh is a very simple one : " Each of the discordant notes leads to and is resolved into that note in the succeeding tonic chord which is nearest to it in pitch, whether that note be above or below it on the scale."

Thus, in the chord , which is resolved into , the F goes to E, and the B to C, the bass note G of course goes to the bass note C (root to root), while the D, being equidistant from C and E, may go to either.

It appears, then, that the only notes (beside the root) which have a compulsory resolution, are the third, B, and the seventh, F. Of these, the "third of the dominant" always goes to the octave of the tonic root, and is therefore called the "leading note," while the seventh always falls to the third of the tonic.

This is a most important rule, and leads to many essential consequences. It should therefore be thoroughly learnt and appreciated at this early stage of the student's progress. We accordingly give a few examples in different keys, by way of illustration :—

8. It would seem that the tendency to a tonic resolution, which, as we have seen, is the characteristic feature of the chord of the dominant seventh, is attributable mainly to the discordant interval which exists between the third and seventh, and which is either a diminished fifth, (if the third be below the seventh,) or an augmented fourth, (if the seventh be below the third,) as may be seen by a careful examination of the preceding examples, where the intervals are purposely placed in various positions.

NOTE. Any interval within an octave is susceptible of what is called "inversion." Which may be thus explained :—

If the lower of the two notes forming any interval be changed into its upper octave, e. g. 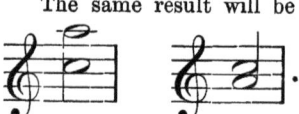 changed to , the interval is said to be inverted, or, in other words,

the new interval thus formed is an inversion of the former: thus if the interval

be given, then its inversion will be

The same result will be obtained if the upper note be taken down an octave: thus—

.

It will be seen by the subjoined table that the *inversions of perfect* intervals are *perfect;* *of major,* are *minor; of minor,* are *major; of augmented,* are *diminished; of diminished,* are *augmented.*

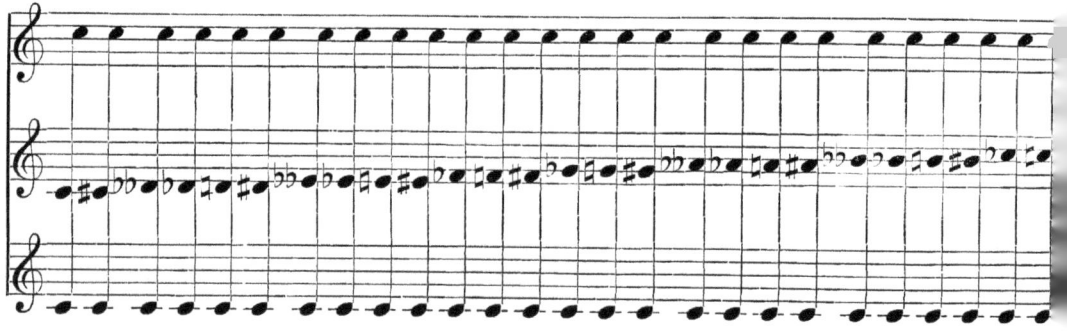

The student is recommended to copy out this list, and name all the upper and lower intervals according to the table given in Chap. I. sect. 6.

Indeed, if a diminished fifth or an augmented fourth be played, alone and unaccompanied, the same craving after resolution will ensue. Thus, if

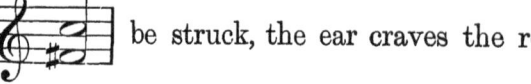 be struck, the ear craves the regular resolution ,

and if the inversion 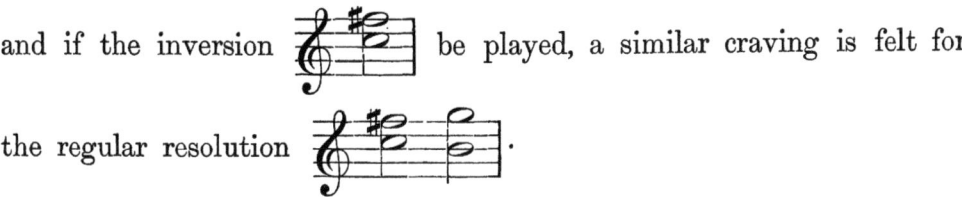 be played, a similar craving is felt for

the regular resolution 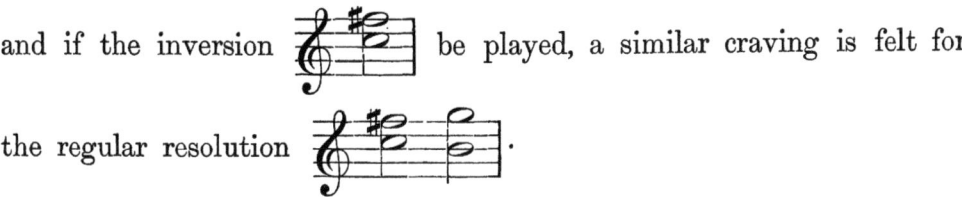 .

This effect, however, is enhanced by the discord which exists between the minor seventh and the root, and more strongly still between the minor seventh and the octave, where the interval of a major second is

produced. Thus  or  .

9. The dominant harmony contains yet another note besides those we have been considering, as will be seen by a reference to Section 3 of this Chapter. It is called the *major ninth*, and it is occasionally added to the chord of the dominant seventh, to strengthen, vary, and enhance its effect, although it is not an essential element of that chord.

When thus enhanced, the complete chord is appropriately called the " chord of the added ninth," or the " chord of the fundamental ninth," to distinguish it from certain other chords of the ninth which will be explained hereafter.

The addition of this new dominant interval to the chord of the dominant seventh does not alter the resolution of the two essential notes of that chord (i. e. the third and the seventh). The third rises to the octave of the tonic root, and the seventh falls to the third of the tonic, just as they would were the ninth absent.

The ninth itself, being as it were a coadjutor and strengthener of the seventh, pursues a similar course to that which is peculiar to that interval. While the seventh falls to the third of the tonic, the ninth falls to its fifth. Thus

Here we see by an example the necessary resolution of the dominant root, the third, the seventh, the ninth; but how about the fifth, D? If the ninth were *not* there, this note might either rise to E, or fall to C, being (nearly) equidistant from both. But the addition of the ninth, A, renders it impossible for the D to proceed downwards to C, without violating that rule of counterpoint which forbids consecutive fifths (see

Chap. I. sect. 8. no. ii.), for their joint progress would be  .

Therefore the fifth of the dominant root (here D) is forced in this case to adopt the alternative of *rising* to the third of the tonic (here E).

To shew this more clearly, we will arrange the notes of the chord in the following position :—

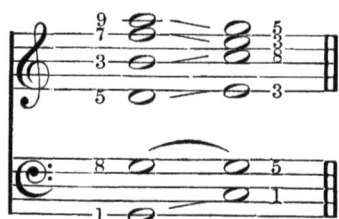

NOTE. Logier does not appear to recognize any dominant interval of harmony beyond the dominant minor seventh. He regards the major and minor dominant ninths as no more than substituted notes.

In this Fétis agrees with him in his valuable Treatise on Harmony.

But this seems to be a very unphilosophical view of the case. For nature supplies us with both these intervals, (the major and minor ninth,) one perfectly, and the other almost perfectly, in tune, as will be shewn hereafter (Chaps. IV and VI), whereas the natural dominant minor seventh is by no means so perfect.

Then again, it is not philosophical to account for an interval by the hypothesis of a substituted note, and yet to allow of the coexistence and simultaneous use of that note and of the one for which it is supposed to be substituted : e. g.

where the A according to these theorists would be substituted for G, and yet the G is allowed to be sounded in another octave.

Surely it is more consistent with analogy, and more agreeable to the phænomena of nature, to regard the ninth here as an *added* harmonic, derived from the chord afforded us by nature,

as will be more fully explained hereafter (vide Chaps. III, IV, VI).

CHAPTER III.

1. FROM what has been already said, it will have appeared that the intervals of a chord may be inverted amongst themselves, and their order of acuteness interchanged, without thereby altering either their relations to the root or to each other.

This may be illustrated by taking the triad or common chord of C, and the chords of the dominant seventh, and of the added ninth, and arranging them variously.

But we may now go a step further, and omit the root altogether, substituting for it occasionally its octave in an upper part.

The effect of this will obviously be that one of the other notes of the chord will be at the bottom of the harmony.

But although the root be in such a case *unheard*, yet it must be always *imagined*.

All the other notes of the chord are equally derived from it, and dependent on it. And the chords thus modified are called inverted chords—or inversions—and their constituent intervals will require the same treatment, for the most part, as though the root were sounded.

The effect on the ear, however, will not be the same, especially in the inversions of the tonic harmony, for the sensation of rest and fixity will be absent : and therefore "every piece of music must end with an un-inverted tonic chord."

2. The tonic triad consisting of three notes, and either of the upper ones being capable of being taken as the lowest note in the harmony, by inversion, as above described, it is clear that only two such inversions are possible—first, when the third is in the bass, and secondly, when the fifth is in the bass.

When the third is in the bass, it is called the "first inversion of the common chord ;" and as the octave of the root then forms the interval of a sixth with the third which is placed in the bass, this chord is also

called the "chord of the sixth." For instance, deriving it from C, , it will appear in the following forms, according to the collocation of the upper notes of which it is composed :

where it may be observed that either the octave of the root or its fifth, (i. e. C, or G,) may be doubled, appearing in two octaves.   Likewise, the G may be left out, but C must not, as it is the characteristic note of the chord.

When the fifth is in the bass, it is called " the second inversion of the common chord," and, as the octave of the root then forms the interval of a fourth with the fifth which is placed in the bass, and as, moreover, the third of the root forms, with this same bass note, the interval of a sixth,—this chord is also called the " chord of the fourth and sixth," or, more concisely, the " chord of the six-four."   For example, taking C as our root as before,   , this chord will appear variously as follows :

This second inversion is less satisfactory than the first, and should be more sparingly employed.

3. And perhaps this will be the most fitting place to introduce the subject of what is known as "thorough-bass-figuring."

This is a kind of musical short-hand, of no great value, but occasionally convenient, by which figures, placed under or over the bass notes of a piece of music, are used to indicate, vaguely but concisely, the kind of harmony to be played with the given bass.

A bass note with no figures attached to it, indicates a simple unaltered triad or common chord. If, however, one of the notes of the harmony has to be modified by an accidental sharp or flat, such modification is indicated by an accidental instead of a figure, (in the case of the third,) or by an accidental added to a figure, (in the case of the fifth). Thus the chords

may be thus expressed

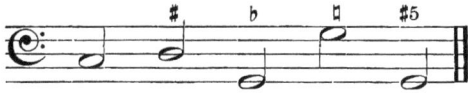

The chord of the dominant seventh is always expressed by the figure 7, either alone or with any accidental natural or flat which it may require. If the fifth or third in the chord require it, accidentals may be used for them as in the case of the common chord. Thus the chords

would be figured as follows :

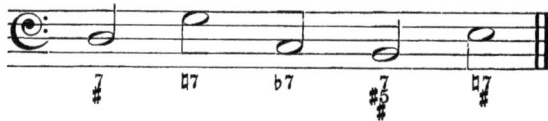

The first inversion of the common chord is figured with a 6. The second inversion of the common chord with a $\frac{6}{4}$. Thus

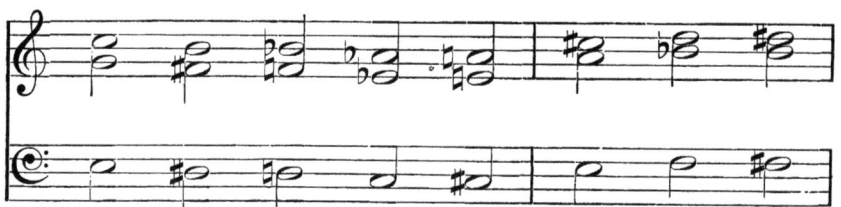

would be indicated as follows :

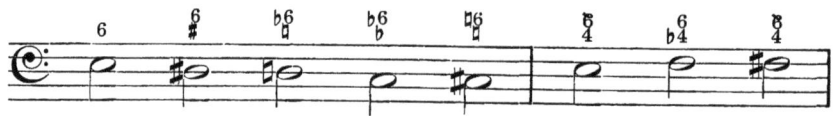

where it should be observed that it is usual to indicate a sharp sixth, fourth, or second by a line drawn through the figure : thus 6, 4, 2.

These symbols are of course perfectly arbitrary, and are merely used for convenience and brevity, and to save an extra stave in certain cases.

4. The chord of the dominant seventh consists, as we have seen, of four notes. It is consequently susceptible of three inversions.

The first inversion has the third in the bass. The octave of the root forms with this bass note the interval of a sixth, the dominant seventh forms the interval of a diminished fifth, and the fifth of the root forms the interval of a third. This chord is called the "chord of the fifth and sixth," or, more concisely, the "chord of the six-five." It is most correct, however, to designate it as the "first inversion of the dominant seventh," to avoid confusion with other chords of similar appearance but different character. It is figured $\frac{6}{5}$, with any accidentals which may be necessary.

The second inversion has the fifth in the bass. The octave of the root forms the interval of a fourth,—the seventh, that of a third,—and the third, that of a sixth,—with the bass note. It is most correctly designated as the "second inversion of the dominant seventh;" but it is also frequently called the "chord of the six-four-three," from the intervals of which it consists. It is figured $\frac{6}{4}$, with whatever accidentals may be requisite. $_3$

The third inversion has the seventh in the bass. The octave of the root forms with this bass the interval of a second; the fifth forms that of a sixth; and the third that of an augmented fourth. It is called properly the "third inversion of the dominant seventh;" but often also the "chord of the six-four-two," or, the "chord of the second and fourth." It is figured $\frac{6}{4}$, with the requisite accidentals. $_2$

We will now give examples of all these inversions, each with its proper thorough-bass figuring :—

Very often it will be a sufficient indication to figure the second inversion $\frac{4}{3}$, omitting the sixth; and to figure the third inversion $\frac{4}{2}$, or even 2 only. This may be done whenever no ambiguity can thence arise.

5. The inversion of a dominant chord does not in anywise change the natural characteristics of the notes of which it is composed. The same rules which held good, therefore, in the resolution of the fundamental chord, in its original condition, will equally hold good in the case of its inversions.

Accordingly, in the first inversion, which has the leading note in the bass, the bass note has a compulsory resolution upwards to the tonic root, while the diminished fifth, which is the minor seventh of the dominant root, is compelled to fall to the third of the tonic. For example—

The second inversion has the fifth in the bass, and consequently this note may either ascend to the third of the tonic or descend to the tonic itself, according to circumstances, the fifth of the dominant having no compulsory resolution. The third in this chord, being the seventh of the root, must of course descend to the third of the tonic; while the sixth, which is the leading note, is compelled to rise to the octave of the tonic root.

The third inversion has the dominant seventh itself in the bass, which is therefore compelled to fall to the third of the tonic. But the third of the tonic in the bass constitutes the first inversion of the common chord : therefore the third inversion of the chord of the dominant seventh must always be followed by the first inversion of the tonic common chord. The augmented fourth in this chord is the leading note, and goes of course to the octave of the tonic root.

In all the inversions, the octave of the dominant root remains without motion, being converted into the fifth of the tonic. The next examples will shew all this more clearly.

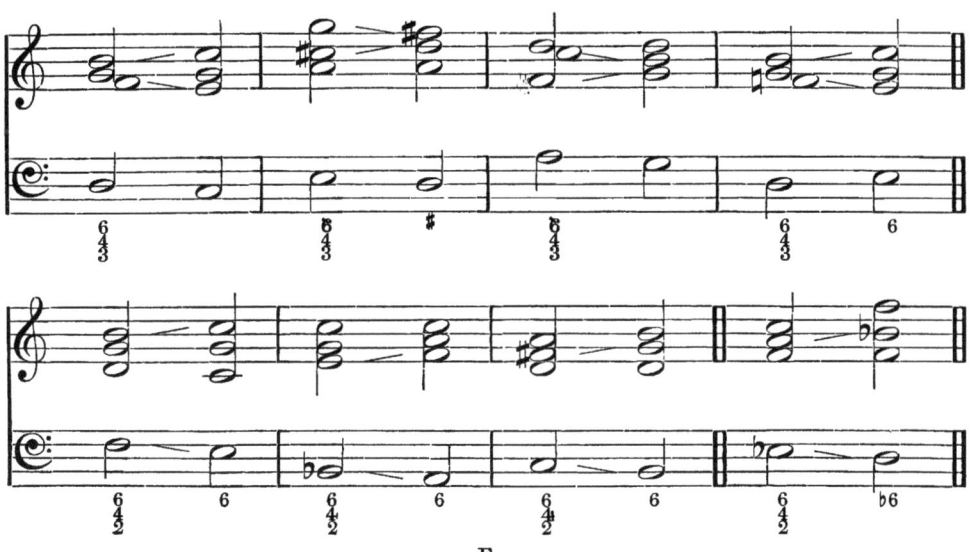

F

We will now give a longer example, including all the inversions of the common chord and the chord of the dominant seventh, with their various resolutions and correct thorough-bass figuring.

The student is recommended to copy this out, and to analyse each chord carefully, putting the letter D over those chords that are dominant, and T over those that are tonic, and drawing lines from all the discordant notes to those which resolve them, according to the foregoing rules.

6. In the chord of the dominant seventh, in its original position, neither the root nor the seventh can be omitted. The leading note may be, on an emergency, but it is always better to avoid this. The fifth may be omitted whenever it is convenient to do so, as it is not an essential note in the chord.

In the first inversion of the dominant seventh the leading note is the bass, and of course cannot be omitted. The seventh of the root, which here becomes a diminished fifth, is the characteristic note, and therefore cannot be spared. The octave of the root, which here is a sixth, may occasionally be omitted; but if this is done, the chord is converted into a diminished triad, and becomes weak and ambiguous, as we shall see hereafter; still, when necessary, it may be omitted. The fifth of the root, which here is a third, may be omitted at pleasure, when convenient.

In the second inversion, the fifth of the root becomes the bass, and cannot be omitted; the fundamental seventh, which is here the third, cannot be omitted, for the same reasons as in the former cases. The leading note, which is the sixth in this inversion, *ought not* to be left out, except when absolutely necessary. But the octave of the root not only may be omitted, but it is generally better that it should be, because of the harsh effect of the interval of a perfect fourth which it makes with the bass.

In the third inversion, the fundamental seventh being in the bass is essential, and must remain. The octave of the root should hardly ever be omitted. The leading note, which forms the augmented fourth, cannot well be dispensed with; but the fifth of the root, which is here a sixth, may be omitted, whenever it is convenient.

These rules about omissions will be found specially useful when the student begins to write music in less than four-part harmony.

Examples of imperfect chords, with the various omissions allowed—

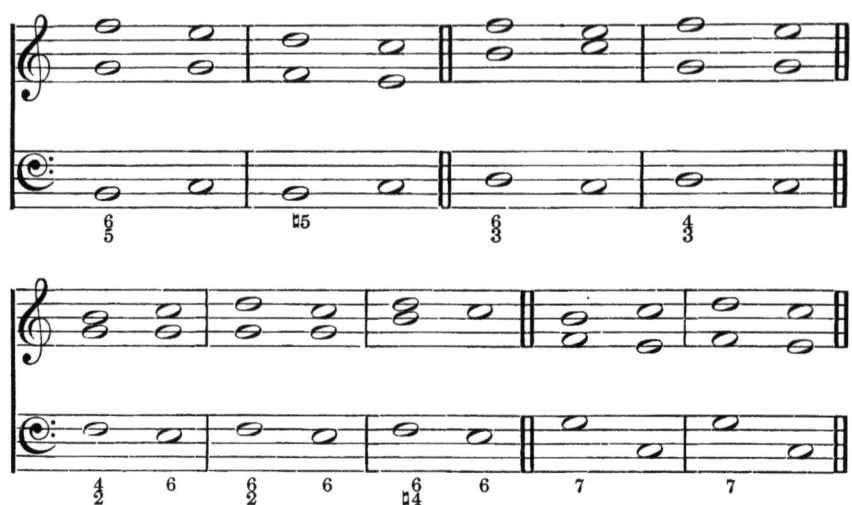

7. It is allowable, and indeed often necessary, to *double* a part, i. e. to let the same note be heard at once in two different octaves.

Now it is obvious that if we thus double a note whose progression is compulsory, we must either break the compelling rule or fall into the great contrapuntal error of consecutive octaves. For instance, if we double

the leading note $\overset{*}{\underset{*}{}}$ 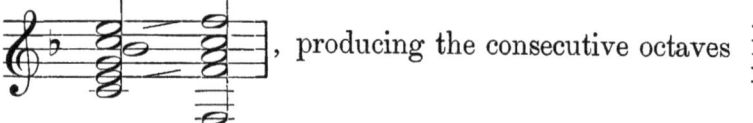, and resolve the chord regularly, both

the notes E will go to F; thus

, producing the consecutive octaves

therefore the first general rule is, that "the leading note and the dominant seventh must not be doubled."

The root and the fifth, however, may be doubled whenever it is convenient.   For the dominant root may either go up a fourth or down a fifth
to the tonic root.   And its octave has, besides this, the power of remaining
without motion.   Moreover, either the root and its octave may also,
under certain circumstances, go to the third of the tonic, though this
is necessarily of very rare occurrence, for contrapuntal reasons.   And
the fifth of the dominant root may either ascend or descend one degree
in its resolution ; when the dominant chord is inverted, moreover, it may
go up or down by a skip to the fifth of the tonic root.

In the second inversion of the chord of the dominant seventh, a licence
is allowed ; namely, that of doubling the fundamental seventh itself, when
the octave of the root is omitted ; and in that case it is considered sufficient for one part, which has this interval, to resolve it regularly by
descending to the third of the tonic : the other, which is the double of
it, may then rise to the fifth of the tonic ; thus—

It is *better* in this case to resolve the *upper* note regularly, and let the
lower one rise instead of falling ; though sometimes even this caution
is not strictly observed.

The fifth of the dominant root may either resolve upwards to the
third of the tonic, or downwards to the tonic itself or its octave.   It
may also go by a skip to the fifth of the tonic, whenever such a progression will not involve consecutive fifths.

The best opportunity for this will be in the third inversion, when the progression of the bass is not to the tonic root, but to its first inversion. The annexed examples will shew the various ways in which the root and the fifth may be doubled—

&c., &c.

8. There is yet one case which remains to be noticed, which is when the chord of the dominant seventh is resolved by the second inversion of the tonic triad, instead of the original common chord of the tonic. This occurs only in the course of a piece of music, never at its close; for the second inversion is no position of rest, but quite the contrary. Example—

The student's ear will at once tell him that something *must* follow this ere rest can be gained.

9. We must now speak of the chord of the added ninth and its inversions.

This chord has five notes in it, and is therefore susceptible of four inversions. It is found, however, in practice, that the fourth of these is seldom available. Still it will be as well to give the whole here, and then to state the cautions and limitations which are required.

The first inversion has the third in the bass; thus

The second inversion has the fifth in the bass; thus

The third inversion has the seventh in the bass; thus

And the fourth inversion has the ninth in the bass; thus

Now it will be perceived, on examining these chords, that all the intervals except the ninth (A) are precisely the same as in the inversions

of the dominant seventh.   Consequently the resolution of these notes is
the same as it is in the former case; except where the new interval of
the added ninth might cause consecutive fifths to occur.   We have already
shewn that such is the case in the original position of the chord of the
added ninth: for if the fifth be resolved downwards to the tonic or its
octave, it makes consecutive fifths with the ninth; thus

Therefore in this case the fifth is of necessity resolved by ascending to
the third of the tonic.   And this holds good also in the inversions.

The first inversion is thus resolved—

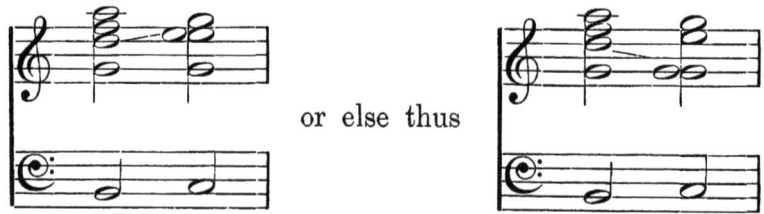

or else thus

(where the D skips downwards to the G).   The latter plan is, on the
whole, preferable.

In the second inversion, the fifth, being in the bass, cannot go to
the tonic root, but is forced to go to the third of the tonic; thus

In the third inversion of course the same resolution must take place, (i. e. to the first inversion of the tonic common chord,) because the dominant seventh is in the bass; thus

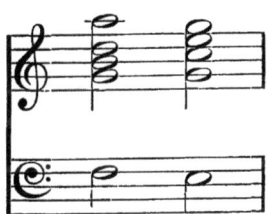

This is perhaps the pleasantest of these inversions, and the easiest to manipulate.

The fourth inversion is crude and harsh, and should be avoided. In it the ninth is in the bass: consequently its natural resolution is into the second inversion of the tonic triad; thus

In this case, the ninth being below the fifth, no consecutive fifths are produced, and therefore the fifths may either ascend or descend.

10. The ninth may go into its resolution before the rest of the chord; thus

or thus—

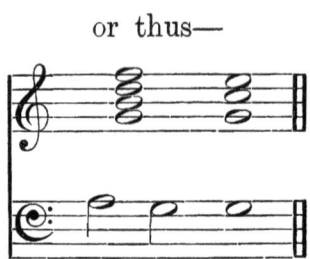

This renders the fourth inversion rather less unwieldy, but still it is very harsh and awkward.

11. Probably this harshness results simply from the fact that the interval of the ninth is not susceptible of regular inversion, as it is beyond the limits of the octave. In the chord of the added ninth, the added note is essentially a *ninth* and not a *second*, seeing that it is originally added on *above the seventh*. Therefore it must always be kept at the distance of a ninth from the root, or the octave of the root, in order to preserve its essential character. But in the fourth inversion of the chord of the added ninth this feature is destroyed by the position of the ninth in the bass. Hence the harshness and awkwardness of this ugly inversion.

12. The thorough-bass figuring of the added ninth is $\frac{9}{7}$. The first inversion is figured $\begin{smallmatrix}7\\6\\5\end{smallmatrix}$; the second $\begin{smallmatrix}6\\5\\4\\3\end{smallmatrix}$; the third $\begin{smallmatrix}6\\4\\3\\2\end{smallmatrix}$; and the fourth $\begin{smallmatrix}7\\6\\4\\2\end{smallmatrix}$; together with any accidental flats or sharps which may be required.

13. The chord of the added ninth is so full of notes, and consequently of dissonances, that it is greatly improved by omissions and curtailments. These must now be considered in order.

When this chord is uninverted, the best note to omit is the *fifth*, both because it is not essential to the character of the chord, and also because by this omission all danger of consecutive fifths with the ninth is avoided; and in the resolution the third of the tonic triad need not be doubled, as it otherwise must be. The *leading note* may also be omitted, as the seventh and ninth are sufficient without it to give a distinctively dominant character to the chord. But neither the *root*, the *seventh*, nor the *ninth* can be omitted.

In the first inversion it is always desirable to omit the *octave of the root*, as this note forms very harsh discords both with the seventh and ninth. The *fifth* may also be omitted freely, for the reasons given before. The *leading note*, being in the bass, is essential, and of course cannot be omitted.

Neither the *seventh* nor the *ninth* of the root can be ever left out.

Note. This rule may perhaps be occasionally relaxed in the case of the *seventh*, when it could not be introduced without contravening the rules of counterpoint. But such licence is not recommended.

In the second inversion, the *fifth*, being in the bass, cannot be dispensed with. The *octave of the root*, however, is better away. The *leading note, seventh,* and *ninth* of the root cannot be omitted.

Note. Here again some relaxation of the rule is sometimes necessitated in the case of the *seventh*. But the chord when thus weakened loses much of its dominant character.

In the third inversion, which has the *seventh* in the bass, (and therefore to be retained as essential,) the *octave of the root* may be omitted, and so may the *fifth*, although the latter omission renders the chord somewhat bare. The *leading note* and the *ninth* can on no account be dispensed with.

In the fourth inversion, which has the *ninth* in the bass, it is almost always necessary to leave out the *octave of the root*; indeed the chord

is hardly ever seen in its complete form, on account of its extreme
harshness. The *fifth* may also be omitted, and even the *seventh* and
leading note, though these two last omissions almost divest the chord
of its dominant character : whichever of these two is omitted, therefore,
the other must always be retained.

The following are the usual forms of this chord, with the omission
of intervals, and with resolution and figuring :—

The chord of the added ninth with the fifth omitted.
All the resolutions in this case are compulsory.

The first inversion, with the octave of the root
omitted. The fifth resolved by a skip, to avoid
consecutive fifths.

NOTE. The leading note is in French called " la note sensible;" and the first inversion of
the added ninth with the octave of the root omitted is therefore called " la septième de sensible." But inasmuch as this designation ignores the true derivation of the chord, it has
not been adopted in this work.

The first inversion, with the fifth of the root
omitted.

The first inversion, with the octave and fifth of the root both omitted.

The first inversion, with the dominant seventh omitted. This should generally be avoided.

The second inversion, with the octave of the root omitted.

The second inversion, with the octave and seventh of the root both omitted. This, however, is not recommended.

The third inversion, with the octave to the root omitted.

The third inversion, with the fifth of the root omitted.

The third inversion, with the octave and fifth of the root both omitted.

The fourth inversion, with the octave of the root omitted. Even thus it is too harsh to be used, except in very rare cases.

The fourth inversion, with the octave and fifth of the root both omitted. This is just tolerable, and may be occasionally used, with caution.

We can also in every case allow the ninth to fall to its resolution before the other notes of the chord. This very much facilitates the use of the fourth inversion. Examples—

&c., &c.

14. Some of the above chords have a strong resemblance, *on paper,* though not when sounded, to the dominant seventh and its inversions. The thorough-bass figuring is also very often similar or identical. It will be as well, therefore, to shew how to distinguish the chords belonging to one series from those which belong to the other.

, which is the first inversion of the chord of the added ninth, with the octave of its root, G, omitted, might at first sight be mistaken for a chord of the dominant seventh on the root B. But the chord of the dominant seventh on B would require D and F to be sharp, not natural, as here, and would be written thus

For in the chord of the dominant seventh the third, or leading note, is always major, and the fifth perfect: whereas in the first inversion of the chord of the added ninth, the third is minor and the fifth diminished.

Again, 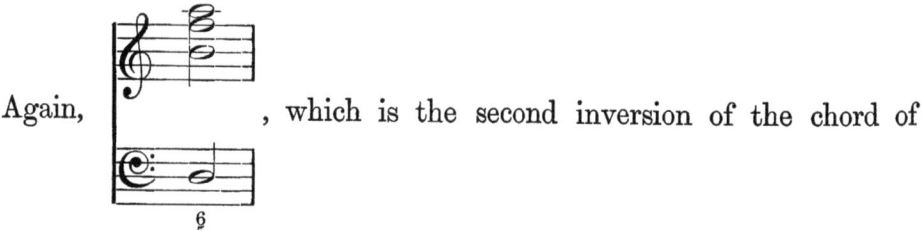 , which is the second inversion of the chord of the added ninth with the octave of its root, G, omitted, might at first sight be mistaken for the first inversion of a dominant seventh on the dominant root B flat. But such a chord would require both the B and the A to be *flattened*, and not natural, as here; thus

For in the first inversion of the chord of the dominant seventh, the sixth is minor and the fifth diminished: whereas in the second inversion of the chord of the added ninth, the sixth is major and the fifth perfect.

Again, 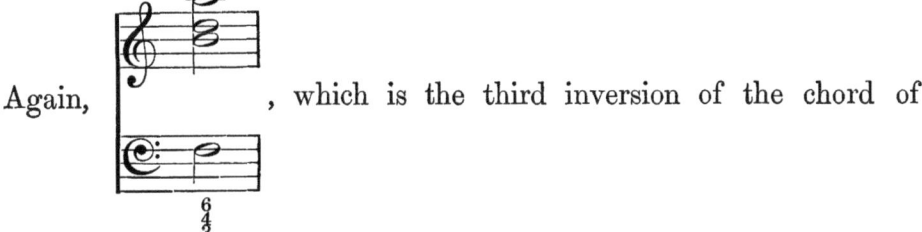 , which is the third inversion of the chord of

the added ninth, with its root, G, omitted, might at first sight be mistaken for the second inversion of a chord of the dominant seventh on the root B flat. But such a chord would require both the B and the A to be *flattened*, and not natural, as here; thus

H

For in the second inversion of the chord of the dominant seventh, the fourth is perfect and the third minor : whereas in the third inversion of the chord of the added ninth, the fourth is augmented and the third major.

Again, 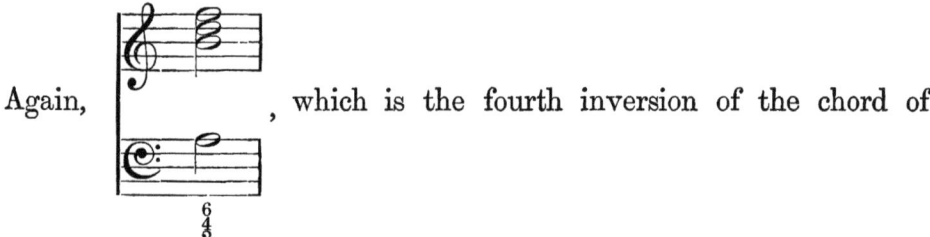 , which is the fourth inversion of the chord of

the added ninth, with its root, G, omitted, might at first sight be mistaken for the third inversion of a chord of the dominant seventh on the root B natural. But such a chord would require both the D and the F to be *sharp*, and not natural, as here ; thus

For in the third inversion of the chord of the dominant seventh, the sixth is major and the fourth augmented : whereas in the fourth inversion of the chord of the added ninth, the sixth is minor and the fourth perfect.

Before going any further, we would strongly recommend the student to transpose all the examples in this Chapter into several other keys. In no other way can he impress all the intervals, chords, and resolutions

so firmly on his memory. We also subjoin a longer example, which he
is advised first to analyse and then to transpose—

H 2

Note. It is needless to give any rules about the doubling of the notes of the chord of the added ninth, as that chord is so full in itself that it seldom admits of such doubling. It may be as well, however, to state that the same rules which were given as to the doubling of notes in the chord of the dominant seventh and its inversions, will equally apply in this case also; with this one addition, that the ninth itself must never on any account be doubled.

We may also remark that it is allowable occasionally to *interchange* dissonant notes in a fundamental discord, provided they afterwards are resolved according to rule, and that the root does not alter while the interchange is being made; for example—

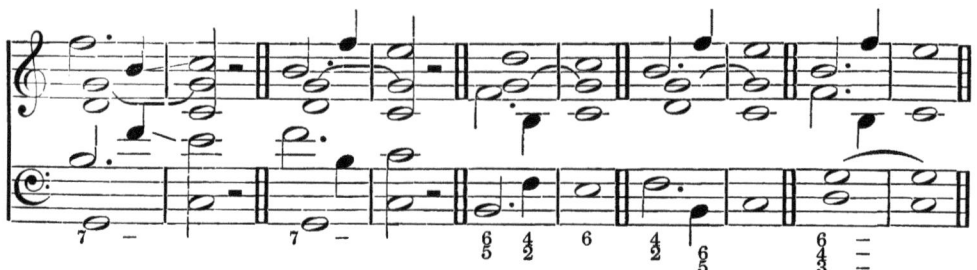

It is always desirable to let the interchanging parts proceed by contrary motion, as here.

Often, too, a licence is granted; a seventh or ninth is allowed to skip to the leading note on the same bass, without any interchange of parts; thus

Nay, more, the seventh may skip sometimes to the fifth on the same bass, instead of being resolved regularly; thus—

though of course this is regarded as a licence.

Another relaxation of the rule is permitted sometimes *when another note on the same bass intervenes between a dissonant interval and its resolution;* thus

15. In thorough-bass figuring it is usual, when a note is resolved on the same bass, to figure the interval to which it passes, even if it be an octave, a fifth, or a third; thus

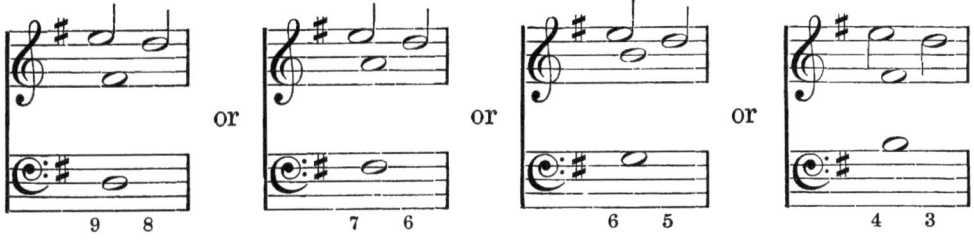

And when the other parts do not move, the fact is usually indicated by horizontal lines drawn from them; thus—

and the same lines are drawn when the bass moves, while the other parts stand still; thus

which last example might also have been figured thus

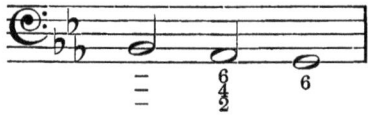

We will now give a figured bass and treble, and the student is to fill in two inner parts, according to the figures, carefully avoiding consecutive fifths and octaves, and scrupulously resolving every dissonance according to the preceding rules:

N. B. The student is advised now to go back to the beginning of Chap. II, and study the sections printed in small type, before he advances any further.

CHAPTER IV.

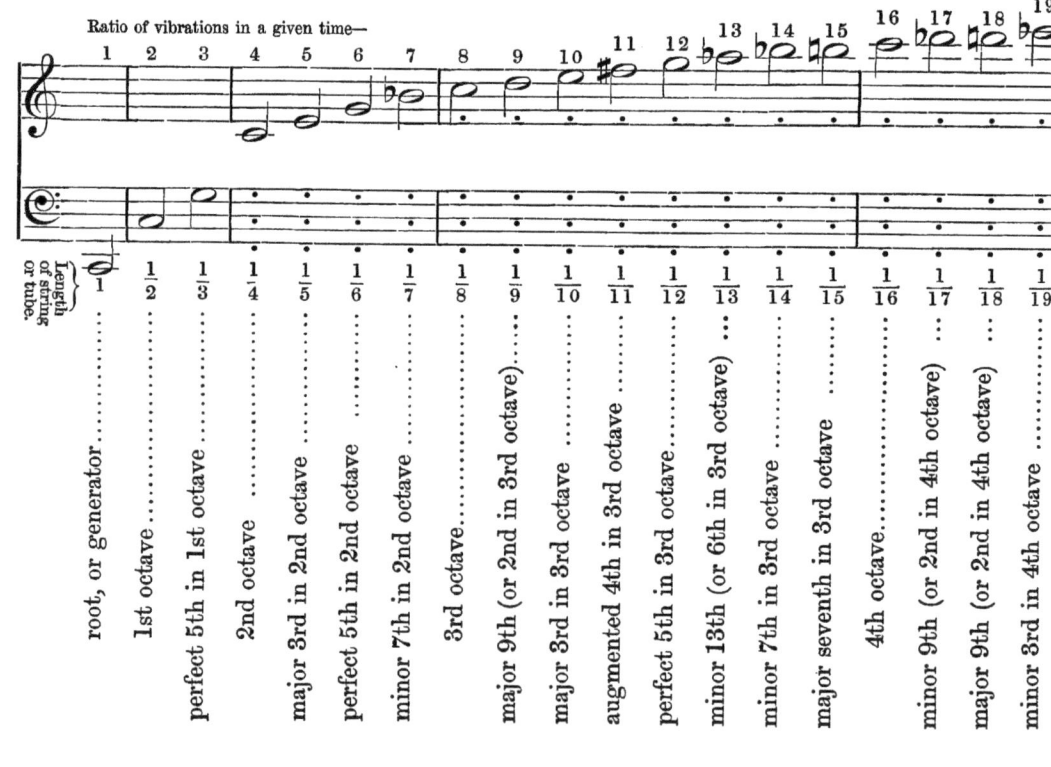

This paradigm of harmonics has been placed at the head of this Chapter, because frequent reference will have to be made to it. The student is advised to study and copy it, as upon it all our superstructure will be built.

2. * In the first place, it will be remarked that in this series of harmonics the distances or intervals between the adjacent notes become progressively less as we proceed upwards.

Thus: the interval between the generator and the first harmonic is an octave—the next interval is a perfect fifth above that—the next is a perfect fourth—the next is a major third—the next a minor third—and so on.

Now, rejecting those sounds which are out of the key, B flat and F sharp, let us take the three notes which come between them, C, D, and E, and we find that they form a real diatonic progression (i. e. the first three notes of the diatonic scale of C major).

Let us then take these three notes as a melody to be harmonized.

For this purpose, the first thing will be to discover the fundamental basses.

Now, seeing that C and E are harmonics of the root C (as above given), and that D is not only so, but is also the second harmonic sound produced by the root G, as we have seen in Chapter II; let us take these sounds, C, G, C, as our basses, and we shall at once effect our object.

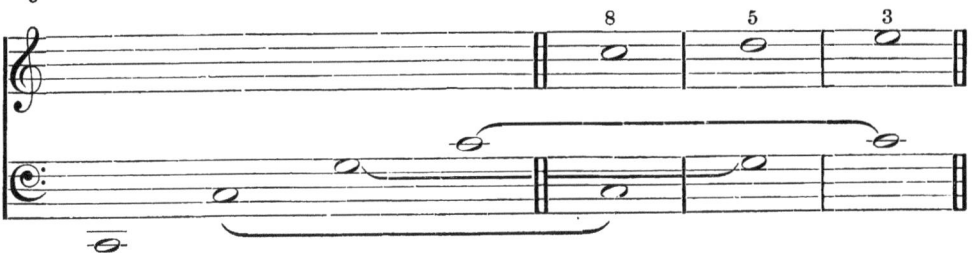

* This section is entirely derived from Logier's admirable " System of the Science of Music ;" London, 1827, pp. 48, et seqq.

I

The fundamental basses being thus discovered, we can now proceed to add harmonies, according to the rules laid down in this book.

Our result is as follows :—

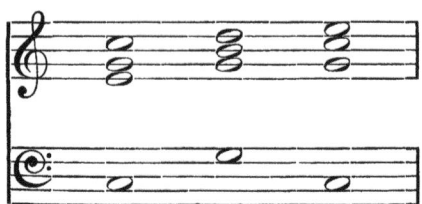

Here, then, we get a harmonized scale of three notes. How are we to get beyond these?

Let us turn to the general paradigm at the head of this Chapter, and we shall find that the harmonic corresponding to no. **7** (or $\frac{1}{7}$ of that string or tube whose whole length would give the generator C) is B flat.

This note is not a part of the scale of C, but it is its fundamental minor seventh; and when it is added to the triad of C, the immediate result is that C ceases to be a tonic root and becomes a dominant.

Then the ear is immediately seized with an irresistible craving after a tonic resolution.

To satisfy this, the seventh must descend and the third must rise, as we have already explained in Chapter II, and thus we find ourselves landed in the key of F.

This process is called a *modulation*, and will be further explained in a future Chapter.

We have by this means added one more note to our original scale of three; and that note is F natural.

Taking F, then, for our new tonic generator, and treating it exactly as we treated C, it will supply three notes, F, G, and A, corresponding to the C, D, and E which we took for our original scale of three notes.

Combining these two series, and connecting them harmonically by means of the dominant seventh, B flat, we shall produce a scale of six notes, or a *hexachord*, as follows :—

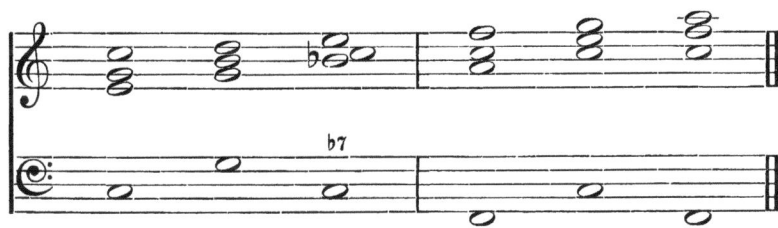

Our scale of melody, taken alone, belongs to the key of C, but our harmonies belong partly to the key of C and partly to that of F.

If we wish to add three more notes according to this system, and by a similar process, we shall modulate into the key of B flat, of which F is the dominant. And in the same way, by pursuing a similar course, we should next modulate into the key of E flat, of which B flat is the dominant. To this process there is no limit.

From these premises Logier * draws the conclusion that " no scale can naturally consist of more than three sounds, for which there are only two fundamental basses required, viz. the tonic and dominant."

He also shews that the " subdominant" (or the fifth below the tonic, or the fourth of the scale ascending) is in reality no true root of any part of a natural scale, but only the generator, or tonic, of a new one.

From all which he sums up the following general rule :—

" Whenever we use a [fundamental] seventh, and thus proceed to a new key, we modulate into that key."

3. From the discoveries in the preceding section, it has been seen how to form a compound scale which shall modulate continually and progressively into new keys : but it has not yet been shewn how to derive from nature a true diatonic scale which shall begin and end in the same key.

As far as the sixth note of the scale, we have to a certain extent succeeded in our endeavour to form and harmonize the scale ; but there we broke away altogether, and hopelessly.

Having wandered into the key of the subdominant, our only way of returning must be by a modulation into the original tonic again.

But, by the above rule of Logier's, this is to be effected by the interposition of the chord of the dominant seventh.

* " System of the Science of Music," pp. 50, 51.

It will be observed here, that at the sixth note of this scale the E flat (or dominant seventh leading to the key of B flat) has not been introduced. The sixth chord may then be considered as a tonic chord, and at rest.

But our object now is not to rest there, but to complete the scale of C in our melody, and at the same time to modulate back from the key of F into that of C by means of the dominant harmony on G. The minor seventh of G, being F, here supplies a combining note for the harmony, (indicated in the above example by a bind,) otherwise these two chords would be totally disjoined.

It will also be remarked that the introduction of the leading note, B natural, in the seventh place of the scale, causes the semitones to fall between the 3rd and 4th, and 7th and 8th, according to the rule of all diatonic major scales.

By this forcible introduction of the dominant harmony of G the ascending major scale of C has been harmonized.

But still there remains an awkward harmonic disconnection between the 6th and 7th of the scale, which can never be entirely got over.

The fact seems to be, that the leading note has so strong a tendency upwards to the octave of the tonic that it cannot bear reference to any lower interval. Its appropriate place would rather appear to be *below* the key-note from which the scale is started,

as then every chord by which the scale is harmonized would be naturally and strongly connected with the next.

If such be a true view, then the leading note would be simply a *preparatory* note, introducing a scale of the compass of a hexachord—ascending. This view of the natural formation of a harmonized ascending scale will be seen to be of some value when we come to consider the minor scale. But that must be reserved for the present.

4. By the use of the inversions of the common chord, and of the chord of the dominant seventh, great variety can be introduced into the harmonic accompaniment of the ascending major scale.

It will be a very useful exercise for the student to take the scale of C and harmonize it according to the following varied basses and figures. And after that he can still further improve himself by transposing his work into other keys.

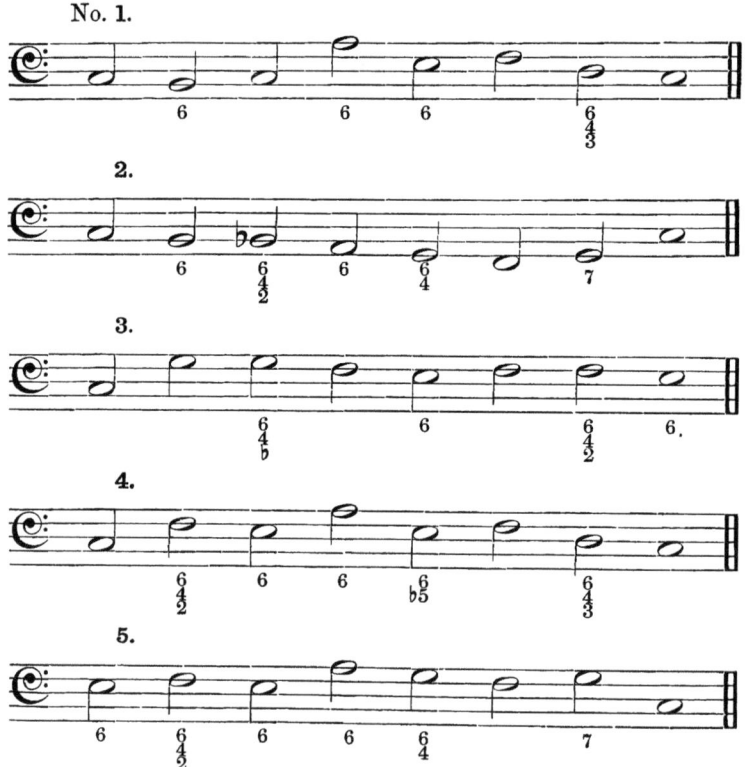

5. The descending diatonic scale now comes for consideration.

Here, of course, the leading note will not help us, as it rises but does not fall. By treating the seventh of the scale as simply part of the common chord of the tonic G, we can get over this difficulty; thus

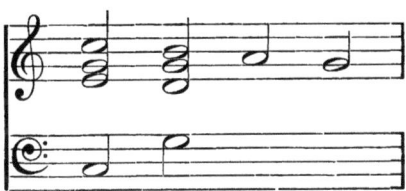

The next stage in our proceedings will be to consider ourselves in the key of G, and to regard the three notes B, A, and G as a natural scale in that key, just as we did with respect to the scale of three notes ascending. Our result will be as follows:—

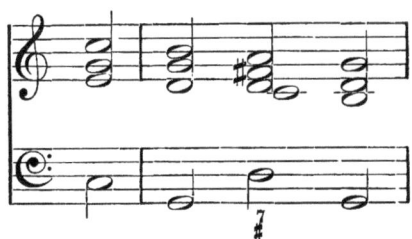

All we require now is a connecting link between these last chords and the three lowest notes of the scale of C, viz. E, D, and C, which notes we shall of course harmonize according to the same method.

Now the fourth note of the scale being F, and F being also the very dominant seventh which we require, let us adopt it, and thus we shall get the descending diatonic scale of C complete, with correct basses and harmonies.

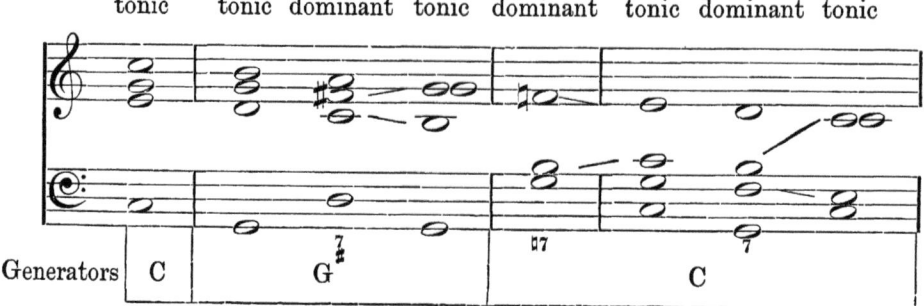

6. Another way of harmonizing this descending scale is by regarding the note A as a part of the chord of the added ninth, in which case the result will be—

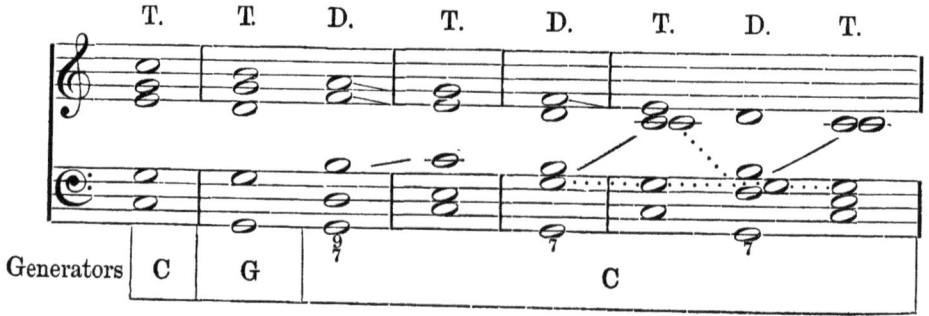

(The lines drawn from note to note indicate the resolutions of discords.)

(The dotted lines indicate the crossing of the parts to avoid consecutive octaves.)

This last method answers best when inversions are used ; thus—

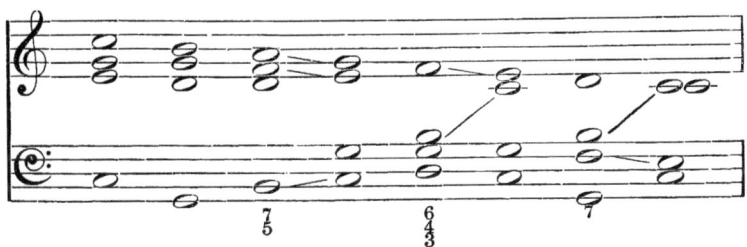

There are many other ways of harmonizing both the ascending and descending diatonic scale, but they involve certain rules of harmony which have not yet been reached in this Treatise, and are therefore for the present postponed.

CHAPTER V.

1. WE must now consider the origin of what is called the "minor mode." Scarcely any subject in the whole science of music has so much perplexed theorists.

The explanation here offered is therefore put forward with some diffidence, although the author is himself convinced of its correctness.

The necessity for such an explanation arises from the conviction that "nothing which is agreeable to the ear can be contrary to nature:" but "the minor mode is agreeable to the ear;" therefore "the minor mode is not contrary to nature"—i. e. it is derived from natural phænomena, and, consequently, can be explained by deductions from those phænomena. In order to render such explanation intelligible, it is necessary here to make a digression, for which, it is hoped, no further apology is needed.

2. Referring to the paradigm of harmonics at the head of Chap. IV, and having regard to those which correspond to prime numbers, i. e. 1, 2, 3, 5, 7, 11, 13, 17, 19, it will appear that their degree of *perfection* gradually decreases as they ascend in pitch, at least so far as No. 13.

To explain this by examples. The octave, or the ratio 1 : 2, is absolutely perfect.

The fifth above this, which is at the distance of a twelfth from the root, or the ratio 1 : 3, is also generally called perfect. And so it is in a certain sense.

But it has one imperfection, viz. that if we continually ascend by intervals of a fifth, we shall never exactly reach an upper octave of the root. For the cycle of twelve fifths, C, G, D, A, E, B, F♯, C♯, G♯, D♯, A♯, E♯, and B♯, is not the same in its results as seven octaves of C: in other words, after reducing the two results to the compass of one octave, it is found that B♯ is sharper than the octave of the root, giving (instead of the ratio 1 : 2) an interval which is represented by $2^{18} : 3^{12}$.

Now, the true octave is in the ratio $1 : 2$, while this interval is $2^{18} : 3^{12}$, or $262144 :$ 531441. The difference, then, between them will be found by comparing these ratios: which is done by multiplying the $1 : 2$ by 262144; i. e. $1 : 2 = 262144 : 524288$: whence it appears that the interval arrived at by ascending in fifths exceeds the true octave by the fraction $\frac{531441}{524288}$, a residuary interval, which is called the "Pythagorean comma."

For this reason all the fifths, in tuning keyed instruments, are tuned a little flatter than perfection, by one twelfth of the Pythagorean comma, an interval so minute that the ear cannot detect it.

The next interval corresponding to a prime number is the major third, which occurs in the second octave, and thus bears the ratio $1 : 5$ to the root.

This interval is much more imperfect than the fifth, and, in tuning a keyed instrument, will require much greater alteration, or *tempering* (as it is called). For the cycle of three major thirds, C, E, G♯, and B♯, falls short of the true octave; giving the ratio $4^3 : 5^3$, instead of the ratio of the octave, $1 : 2$, which exceeds it by the comma $\frac{128}{125}$, or "enharmonic diesis."

This imperfection is obviously much more appreciable than that of the fifth, especially when it is remembered that in "tempering" it has to be equally distributed among no more than three major thirds.

The next prime number in the series (no. 7) gives the interval of the fundamental minor seventh. But, as has been already observed, it gives it very much too flat. So much so, that most theorists have demurred to accepting it as the origin of dominant discords and of modulation.

Rameau *, who, I believe, first noticed it among the acute harmonics of a vibrating string, called it "le son perdu," the lost sound, and passed it over as insignificant.

But, even in the last century, there were some writers who to a certain extent recognized its place in the harmonic system†.

It is admitted by Chladni ‡ to be midway between consonances and dissonances, although he deprecates its use.

He, however, uses these remarkable words: "On peut cependant présumer que la cause, pour laquelle l'accord le la septième, (ut, mi, sol, si♭), et celui de la sixte superflue, (ut mi, sol, la♯), ne sont pas aussi désagréables à l'oreille, que l'on pourrait le croire, d'après leurs

---

* " Génération Harmonique;" Paris, 1737, (vide Chap. i.)

† Vide *Pizzati*, " La Scienza de' Suoni e dell' Armonia;" Venice, 1782, (Part. IV, Chap. ix.)   Also *Tartini*, "Trattato di Musica;" Padua, 1754, (p. 126.)

‡ "Traité d' Acoustique;" Paris, 1809, (p. 28.)

nombres compliqués, tient à ce que l'oreille substitue à ces nombres les rapports 4 : 5 : 6 : 7, dans lesquels l'intervalle $\frac{7}{4}$ diffère de la septième $\frac{16}{9}$ du comma $\frac{64}{63}$, et de la sixte superflue du comma encore plus petit $\frac{126}{125}$." But surely, as we admit of the temperament of fifths and thirds, without denying the genuineness of those found in nature, so we may regard the ordinary minor seventh as a tempered modification of the fundamental seventh found among the harmonic sounds of nature.

Similarly, we may regard the harmonics corresponding to the prime numbers 11 and 13 in our paradigm as *representing* the augmented fourth and the minor sixth in the third octave :—although the former is much too flat, being nearly midway between the perfect and augmented fourth ; and the latter is much too sharp, being also intermediate between the major and minor sixth.

The next prime number, 17, however, gives us the interval of a minor ninth, very nearly in tune, being only a very little too flat, and almost identical with that interval on an equally tempered instrument*. This number, then, we may at once admit among our fundamental discords, and use as freely as the major ninth or the minor seventh.

The next prime number is one of the utmost importance (No. 19), as it gives us the *minor third of nature*, and may be regarded as the source of the whole system of the minor mode.

It is almost in tune. Indeed it is *more satisfactory to the ear* than the minor third as usually represented by the ratio 5 : 6.

Reducing it to the first octave, it is represented by the ratio 16 : 19, and only falls short of the usual ratio 5 : 6 by the very small comma $\frac{96}{95}$.

Regarding the major triad as 16 : 20 : 24, and the minor triad, as here derived, as 16 : 19 : 24, nothing can be more simple and natural than their relations one to the other. Even Chladni admits this †, where he says " Peutêtre quand on se sert quelquefois de l'accord parfait mineur au lieu du majeur, ou du majeur au lieu du mineur, l'oreille est *moins blessée*(!) parce qu'elle substitue à la tierce mineur $\frac{5}{6}$ l'intervalle $\frac{19}{16}$, en entendant une variété de rapports, comme 16 : 19 : 24, et 16 : 20 : 24."

Let us, then, assume the fundamental minor third of nature to be $\frac{19}{16}$, or that produced by taking $\frac{16}{19}$ of the length of a string or tube.

It will only remain to shew why the usual figures, 5 : 6, cannot be taken for this pur-

---

* This derivation of the minor ninth is duly recognized by Catel, in his well-known " Traité d' Harmonie ;" Paris, 1802, (p. 6.)

† *Chladni*, " Traité d' Acoustique ;" (p. 29.)

pose—in other words, why the minor triad is not correctly represented by the ratios 10 : 12 : 15.

3. Referring once more to our general paradigm at the head of Chap. IV, and seeing which are the notes represented therein by the ratios 10, 12, and 15, we find them to be E, G, and B, or the minor triad of E. But the root of all the notes in this series is C, not E. And C cannot be the root of the minor triad of E. Therefore the numbers 10, 12, and 15 do not correctly produce a genuine minor triad. Therefore the ratio 10 : 12 (or, which is the same, 5 : 6), does not represent a real fundamental minor third.

But it *does* really give the interval between the third and fifth of the major triad, as the paradigm will shew.

There are, then, in nature two different minor thirds, only one of which is fundamental; or, as it may be expressed, one of them, $\frac{19}{16}$, is the root with its minor third, the other, $\frac{6}{5}$, is the third and fifth with the root omitted.

4. It may, then, from these arguments, be fairly assumed that the minor triad has its origin in nature, analogously to the major, and that it is part of the tonic series.

The dominant must always have its third or leading note major; otherwise it would be too far from the note to which it leads, and from which it is necessarily a semitone distant.

5. On referring to Chapter I, it will be seen that every major key has a minor key connected with it, called its "relative minor." This connection can hardly be said to be of natural origin, inasmuch as the harmonics of the root of the major key do not give us the common chord of its relative minor. But as several of the intervals of their scales are common to both, and as their "signature" (or the flats or sharps in the stave) is the same, and as, moreover, it is very easy and very usual to go either by modulation or by harmonic progression, (which term shall be explained hereafter,) from one to the other; it will be most

convenient on the whole to illustrate the derivation and harmonization
of the minor mode by starting from the key-note A, and taking as our
model the process adopted for the scale of C major in the preceding
Chapter.

6. For this purpose we will shew the scale of three notes in the
major and minor modes, side by side—

Now although these two scales *look* very similar at first sight, 'yet
are they essentially unlike ; and the minor sounds eminently unsatisfactory.

The reason of this is, that the harmony of the second note of the
major scale is essentially *dominant*, seeing that it will admit of the
addition of a *seventh ;* thus—

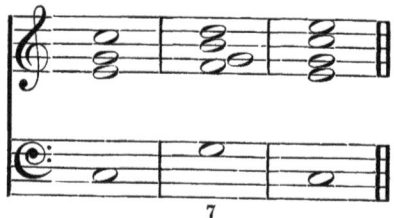

whereas the harmony of the second note of the minor scale, as written
here, is not, and cannot be, dominant, inasmuch as it contains no leading
note, the third being minor. It is simply the minor triad of E, and has
no connection with the chords with which it is here associated.

To correct this, it is merely necessary to put a sharp before the G, when it immediately becomes a leading note :—

to which we may add the seventh if we please—

In forming the harmonized major scale, the first three notes were followed by three others, similar, and similarly harmonized, in the key of the subdominant. Pursuing the same course, as far as possible, with the minor scale, the result will be as follows—

This will do very well. But it differs from the scale in the major, inasmuch as there is no modulation into the key of D between the third and fourth note. This is inevitable, because the third note of the scale is necessarily a minor third to the root A, and therefore cannot be used as part of a dominant chord. Still, there is sufficient connection to satisfy the ear, and a real modulation does take place at the next note, where the leading note, C♯, is introduced.

As we have thus got out of the key of A into that of D minor, we are obliged to modulate back again to our original key: and this obliges us to introduce the leading note, G♯, into the melody as the seventh note of the scale. The whole will then stand as follows—

It will not escape notice, that between the sixth and seventh notes of the minor scale, as here shewn, there is the interval of an augmented second. This constitutes the chief characteristic of a regular minor scale.

7. In Chapter IV, towards the end of section 3, it is shewn how awkwardly the sixth and seventh notes of the diatonic scale hang together. This is even more apparent in the minor scale, in consequence of the introduction of the very dissonant interval of the augmented second between those notes. If the leading note be, as it were, prefixed to the minor hexachord (or scale of six notes), all this awkwardness vanishes at once; thus—

Every chord connects itself with those next it, without difficulty, and without harshness. There is therefore no small reason to surmise that this is the most natural form of the scale.

8. Before proceeding to harmonize the descending minor scale, it will be necessary to introduce a new dominant interval, or fundamental discord—the *minor ninth*. This is one of the most important elements of modulation, and affords a greater variety of resources than any other known combination of notes to the experienced harmonist. It will be well, therefore, to devote a Chapter to it alone.

CHAPTER VI.

1. IT will be seen on reference to the paradigm prefixed to Chapter IV, that the 17th harmonic gives us the minor ninth in the fourth octave from the root. It is therefore a natural harmonic.

But it is clearly no part of the tonic harmony, for it is out of the key. Nor is it in the *key* of the dominant; for the minor ninth, for example, of the dominant G is A flat, which neither belongs to the scale of G nor to that of C major.

But it *does* belong to the scale of C *minor*, although it is a harmonic of the dominant G.

It therefore is a very important addition to the dominant harmony, because it only belongs to it as such, and by no means belongs to the same root considered as a tonic, being necessarily and essentially dominant, and leading downwards to the fifth of the tonic quite as irresistibly as the leading note leads upwards to the octave of the tonic, or the dominant seventh downwards to its third.

When the tonic is of the minor mode, the force of the dominant seventh is weakened, because, instead of falling a semitone to its resolution, it has to fall a whole tone, since the tonic third is minor. Compare the two—

semitone   whole tone

But the minor ninth at once makes up for this defect, by its own strong dominant tendency to the fifth of the tonic.

The two together form as strong a dominant chord as can be required. And the additional indication of the minor mode which this interval gives, renders it of especial value when we wish to introduce and fix that mode.

The major ninth is not suitable for the minor mode, on account of its incongruity with the sixth note of the minor scale, which is minor, as we have seen, and with that same note considered as the third of the subdominant triad, which, as we have also seen, is minor also. Therefore the minor ninth must be substituted for the major in the minor mode.

Its resolutions, inversions, and figuring are analogous to those of the chord of the added major ninth, only that the accidental flats and sharps involved will of course be different; and in this difference there is also this advantage, i. e. that there is no danger of mistaking the inversions or figuring of the chord of the minor ninth for those of the dominant seventh; for in the former the accidentals are always combined *of a contrary kind**, which is never the case in the latter.

A few examples will shew all these points at one view.

The chord of the minor ninth uninverted, properly resolved and figured.

The same, with the ninth resolved to the octave on the same bass, before the resolution of the other parts.

The next two examples give the ninth in an inner part, and below the leading note. This is always allowable with the minor ninth, and gives it a great advantage over the major,—where such a position is not recommended.

* i. e. sharps against flats; thus is easily to be distinguished from or .

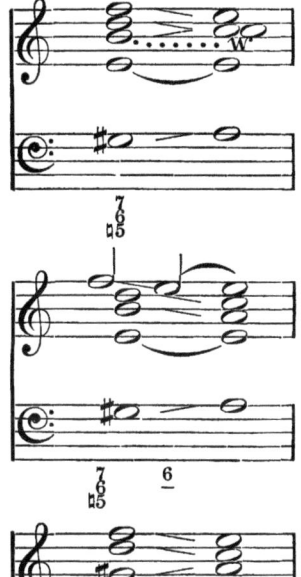

The first inversion of the chord of the minor ninth,—where observe the forced movement of the fifth B up to C, to avoid consecutive fifths. As, however, one of the fifths is *diminished*, this precaution is sometimes neglected by modern composers.

The same, with the ninth resolving before the rest. Here the progression of the fifth is perfectly free and safe.

The second inversion. Here the fifth, being in the bass, must not descend to the tonic, as the consecutives would be between the extreme parts, and therefore offensive.

or,

When the ninth is resolved in this way, the hidden consecutives between the extreme parts *may* be tolerated (as in bar 2), but it is very much better as in bar 1.

This method of resolution takes away all difficulty about the descent of the bass. It may equally apply to the first inversion if required.

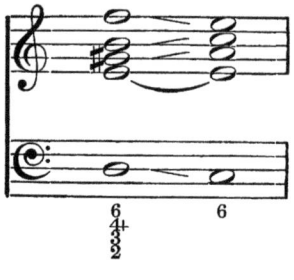

The third inversion, regularly resolved.

The same, with the ninth resolved before the rest.

The same, resolved so as to enable the fifth to descend.

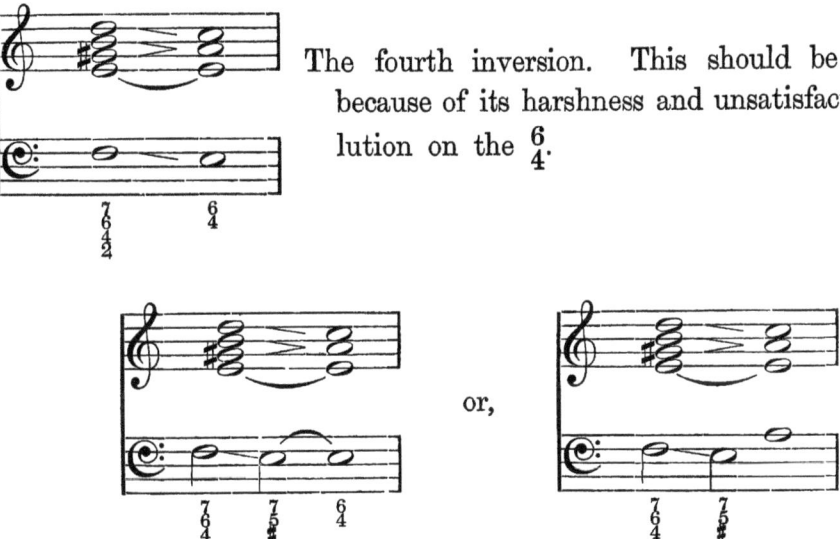

The fourth inversion. This should be avoided, because of its harshness and unsatisfactory resolution on the $\frac{6}{4}$.

or,

Two ways are here shewn of improving the resolution of this ugly chord. The former is not very satisfactory, but the latter is good. In this inversion, the ninth being below the fifth, no consecutive fifths can occur.

2. Hitherto we have been speaking of the chord of the minor ninth and its inversions, without omitting any interval. Like the chord of the added ninth, however, (see Chap. III. 13,) this chord is all the better for such curtailment; and the general rules for the omission of its various intervals in each inversion are similar to those given in the case of the chord of the added ninth.

But when the octave of the root is omitted from the chord of the minor ninth, a very remarkable and important series of chords is discovered, which demand special consideration.

3. The first inversion of the chord of the minor ninth, omitting the octave of the root, is known as the " chord of the diminished seventh," and is so named after its characteristic interval—

It is susceptible of three inversions, all of them being of the greatest use in harmonizing—

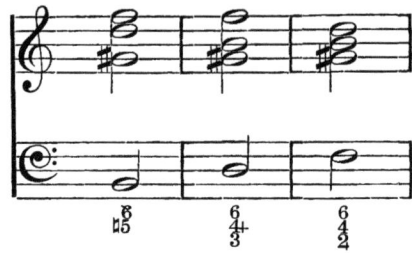

Now on examining the chord of the diminished seventh, it will be seen that it consists entirely of minor thirds superposed—G♯B, BD, and DF. And on examining the inversions, they will be found to consist in each case of two minor thirds and one augmented second; thus—BD, DF, and FG♯; DF, FG♯, and G♯B; and FG♯, G♯B, and BD.

On all keyed instruments, the same key stands for G♯ and A♭. And although they are not the same note *really*, yet they are so nearly the same that one may be always substituted for another with impunity. Indeed, the construction of our instruments, the method of tuning now universally prevalent, and the requirements of free modulation, render such interchanges imperatively necessary.

NOTE. The interval which actually exists between two such notes is named the " Enharmonic Diesis," and is represented by the fraction $\frac{128}{125}$.

See short Examples at the end of this work, Nos. 6, 7, and 12.

Any note, then, may be changed into that which is nearest it in pitch, and which is represented by the same key on all keyed instruments, e. g. G♯ into A♭, A♯ into B♭, B♯ into C♮, C♯ into D♭, D♯ into E♭, E♯ into F♮, F♯ into G♭; and conversely, G♭ into F♯, F♭ into E♮, E♭ into D♯, D♭ into C♯, C♭ into B♮, B♭ into A♯, A♭ into G♯.

This sort of interchange is called an "*Enharmonic Change.*" The ear is, as it were, deceived by it, just as it is by the tempering applied to the fifths, thirds, and sevenths, as described in Chapter V. Whence it follows that the chord of the diminished seventh and all its inversions may be alike regarded as in fact composed of three minor thirds; thus—

1st minor third {	F	G♯ or A♭	B or C♭ or B	D or E♭♭
	D	F F	A♭ A♭ or G♯	B or C♭
2nd minor third {	D	F F	A♭ A♭ or G♯	B or C♭
	B	D D	F F or E♯	G♯ or A♭
3rd minor third {	B	D D	F F or E♯	G♯ or A♭
	G♯	B B	D D or C×	E♯ or F

The minor thirds may also be reckoned the other way—

(1)   F to G♯ or A♭;

(2)   G♯ or A♭ to B or C♭;

(3)   B or C♭ to D or E♭♭; &c.

For every one of the intervals composing this chord may be enharmonically changed, as is here shewn.

M

Hence it may be seen how very useful this chord is in modulating from key to key. For example—

In this example—

Bar i. contains the minor triad of A, and the first inversion of the dominant triad of E, with the seventh omitted.

Bar ii. contains the minor triad of A; and the third inversion of the chord of the minor ninth of A without the octave of the root: being therefore the second inversion of the chord of the dimi-nished seventh, leading to the next chord.

Bar iii. contains the first inversion of the minor triad of D ; and the first inversion of the chord of the minor ninth of A, without the octave of the root—being the chord of the diminished seventh.

Bar iv. contains an enharmonic alteration of the last chord, whereby it is converted into the fourth inversion of the minor ninth of C, without the octave of the root—being therefore the third inversion of the chord of the diminished seventh. In the last half of the bar, the bass resolves the minor ninth by descending to the root, and the rest of the chord remains as a chord of the dominant seventh on C.

The student will now be able to carry on this process of analysis, by the aid of the rules already given. He is begged, however, to take especial notice of the enharmonic change in bar vi., which he will have to examine very carefully. He will do well, also, to observe the roots and keys, as indicated in capital letters below the bass stave.

4. In bar x. of the preceding example, the common chord of E major is marked thus †. This has been done to draw attention to the fact that here the chord of the minor ninth has been followed by a *major* triad. This licence is always *allowable;* although the character of this chord is more essentially minor than major, as has been sufficiently shewn. By means of this licence, an even more extended usefulness is gained, and the composer is enabled by it to modulate still more freely.

5. It is then possible from one chord of the diminished seventh to modulate directly into a great variety of keys: for instance, taking

our start from A minor, the following resolutions of the diminished

seventh $\begin{smallmatrix} F \\ D \\ B \\ G\sharp \end{smallmatrix}$ will at once appear :—

A major   C minor   C major

F♯ minor   F♯ major   D♯ major

D♯ minor   E♭ minor   E♭ major

G♭ major   G♭ minor

At †, bars viii. and ix., the equivalent notes have been omitted, and the enharmonic change taken for granted. This is the usual way of writing such modulations, for the sake of simplicity.

We may here quote a very good example from Catel (Traité d'Harmonie), which clearly exhibits the enharmonical resources of the chord of the diminished seventh—

In this example the diminished seventh ∗ and all its inversions are successively presented in bars ii.—vi., and all the various roots given from which they are severally derived. Yet, if played on a keyed instrument, the chords in these five bars remain unchanged, as will be at once perceived on playing them.

6. Before proceeding any further, it will be well to give a rule by which to discover the root of any fundamental harmony.

For this purpose it will be necessary to refer to the general table of the keys with their signatures, given in Chapter I, sect. 5.

Now, it will be found a convenient plan, to class the key-notes according to their signatures, calling that key the sharpest key which has the greatest number of sharps; and, generally, in comparing two or more keys together, calling that the sharpest which has the most sharps or the fewest flats in its signature.

And we may apply the same mode of speaking to the individual notes themselves: for instance, E♮ may be called a sharper note than D♮, because the signature of that key of which it is the tonic has two more sharps than belong to the key of D.

Similarly, F may be called a sharper note than B♭; and, generally, we may call the notes in the subjoined list sharper or less sharp according to the order in which they stand; those to the left hand being sharper than those to the right. Thus, in the list of notes—

C♯, F♯, B, E, A, D, G, C, F, B♭, E♭, A♭, D♭, G♭, C♭;

C♯ is the sharpest of all notes; then comes F♯, and so on, decreasing in sharpness till we reach C♭, which is the flattest of all.

This is simply a convenient mode of naming the various notes by way of comparison, the special advantage of which we shall now proceed to shew.

7. "In every fundamental chord, the leading note is the sharpest note to be found."

To this rule there is no exception, and by means of it the root of every fundamental chord can easily be found.

For example, let us try to discover the root of the following chord—

On reference to the list or table in the last section, it will be seen that of the notes composing this chord the sharpest is A; therefore A is the leading note; therefore F is the root; and it is evidently the first inversion of the chord of the minor ninth without the octave of the root, otherwise called the chord of the diminished seventh. And from this it follows, in the regular course, that the chord belongs to the key of B♭ minor.

This rule is so compendious, so simple, and of such general application, that it ought to be thoroughly mastered, and continually applied, by every student of harmony.

To it may also be added the following subsidiary rule—

" If there is a minor ninth in any chord, that ninth will be the flattest note."

Thus, in the above example the flattest note is G♭, which is thereby known to be the minor ninth of F, the root.

If, however, there be no minor ninth in a dominant chord, then the flattest note will be the dominant seventh.

Thus, in the annexed chord, the flattest note is D, which is the dominant seventh of E, and the whole chord is a chord of the added ninth on that root:

8. Let us now apply these rules to the enharmonic variations of the chord of the diminished seventh and its inversions—

In No. i. the sharpest note is C♯, therefore the root is A♮, and the chord is a diminished seventh ♭7 ♮5.

In No. ii. the sharpest note is E♮, therefore the root is C♮, and the chord is in its last inversion ♮4 6 2.

In No. iii. the sharpest note is A♯, therefore the root is F♯, and the chord is the first inversion of a diminished seventh ♮4 6 3.

In No. iv. the sharpest note is G♮, therefore the root is E♭, and the chord is the second inversion of a diminished seventh ♮5 6 ♭.

In the first case the chord leads to D minor (or major); in the second

to F minor (or major) ; in the third to B minor (or major) ; and in the
fourth to A♭ minor (or major).

The student will now analyse the following exercise, detecting the
roots, and describing every chord—

Note. If the root and leading note be both omitted from the chord of the minor
ninth, it is reduced to an imperfect or diminished triad—

N

In this form it is impossible to detect its root, except by a consideration of the succeeding chord.

If that chord be on the tonic A, the preceding example will of course be an imperfect chord of the minor ninth on the dominant root E.

$$E \qquad A$$

But if the succeeding chord be on the tonic C, then the doubtful chord must be regarded as an imperfect chord of the dominant seventh on G.

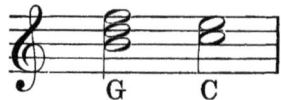

$$G \qquad C$$

It is therefore the most equivocal and unsatisfactory of all the simple chords in music.

CHAPTER VII.

1. HAVING introduced and explained the chord of the minor ninth and its derivatives in the last Chapter, we may now proceed to apply it to the harmonization of the descending minor scale.

In Chapter V, section 6, the ascending minor scale was worked out: and it was shewn in the following section, that between the sixth and seventh degrees of this scale the chromatic interval of an augmented second occurs.

In forming and harmonizing the descending minor scale, care will be required in the treatment of this awkward interval.

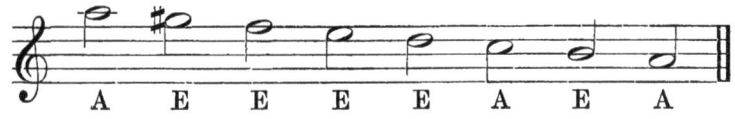

A   E   E   E   E   A   E   A

On setting out the melody, it will be observed that all the notes of it belong to the dominant chord of E, except the first, sixth, and eighth. We need not, then, unless we choose, have any dealings with the subdominant D, or with any harmony but that of the tonic and dominant.

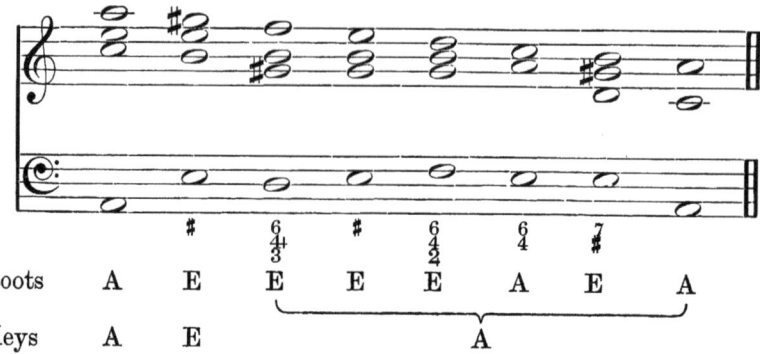

Roots	A	E	E	E	E	A	E	A
Keys	A	E			A			

But here there appears a somewhat irregular treatment of the dominant seventh between the third and fourth chords; thus—

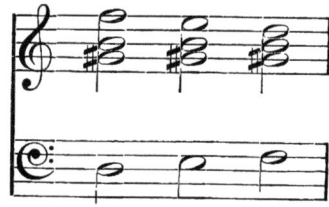

And although this progression is *tolerated* by licence, on account of the contrary motion between the extreme parts, yet it is by no means elegant.

It will therefore be better to look on the note E in this scale as part of the tonic harmony, and to harmonize thus—

Roots	A	E	E	A	E	A	E	A
Keys	A	E			A			

Or, if we prefer to introduce the subdominant triad D, we can do so with good effect, as follows—

| Roots | A | E | E | A | D | A | E | A |
| Keys | A | E | | A | D | | A | |

And this can be varied by using different inversions.

On the sixth chord we shall have some observations to make in a subsequent Chapter, as, in such cases as this, it is not, strictly speaking, so much an inversion of the tonic triad, as a double dissonance by suspension; on which see Chapter VIII, section 7.

2. It is often convenient to alter the minor scale, so as to avoid the augmented second between its sixth and seventh degree. This is usually done by sharpening the sixth in ascending, and by flattening the seventh in descending.

The scale then departs from nature, and becomes entirely artificial. It will then stand thus—

Such an alteration necessitates a total change in the harmonization. The following appears to be the best method :—

3. It will be useful now to give examples of the harmonizing of scales minor and major when the scale is given to the bass part. As an exercise to the student, only the bass and figures will be given, and it will be for him to supply the three upper parts, and to assign the proper roots of each chord :

CHAPTER VIII.

1. All the discords hitherto described have belonged to one class, viz. "fundamental discords." That is, they have all been parts of the dominant harmony, as derived from nature. But besides the fundamental discords, there are others of various kinds, some of which it is time to explain.

2. It may be well, in this place, before going further, to define a few terms more accurately than has yet been done in this Treatise.

i. A *Concord* is a combination of root, third, and fifth, such as the major and minor triads—(and perhaps their inversions also, though they are imperfect concords).

ii. The sounds of which a concord consists are called *Consonances*.

iii. When any one of the sounds composing a concord is removed, and some other sound substituted in its place, the perfection and satisfactoriness of the concord is destroyed, and a different and contrasting effect produced. The intruded new sound which produces this result is called a *Dissonance*.

iv. The chord in which the dissonance is heard is called a *Discord*.

3. The discords and dissonances of fundamental dominant harmony have been discussed. It is necessary now to speak of *Dissonances by Suspension* *.

Let the following melody be played, accompanied only by its fundamental bass. It is satisfactory to the ear, though tame and bald:

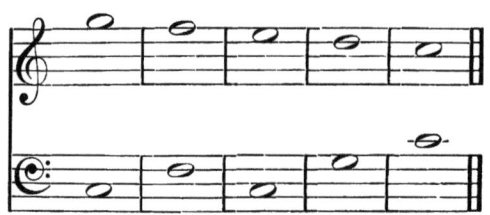

But let the sound G in the melody be continued through part of the succeeding bar, without altering the bass (as in the following example), and the ear will immediately begin to long for the delayed note F. And if each note in this melody be similarly treated, we shall have

When an interval of a melody (or of an inner part) is thus kept back in *descending*, it is called a suspension.

Thus, in the preceding example,

G suspends F,

F suspends E,

E suspends D.

* This is principally derived from Logier's "System," ut sup. pp. 62-65.

Or, if viewed in relation to their bass notes,

The ninth suspends the eighth,
The fourth suspends the third,
The sixth suspends the fifth.

These include all the *dissonances by suspension.*

The following are examples of each :—

Here the dissonance of the fourth is produced by suspending the third.

Here the dissonance of the ninth is produced by suspending the eighth.

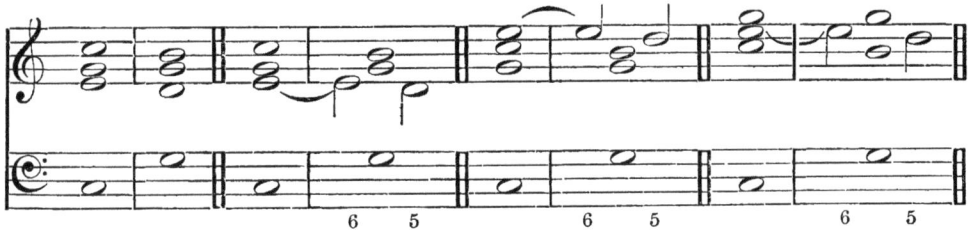

Here the dissonance of the sixth is produced by suspending the fifth.

O

4. The suspension, then, being produced by a lagging note—a note behind the rest in the progression from one chord to another,—it follows that these dissonant notes must exist as consonances in the previous chord, before they became dissonances by being, as it were, left behind.

The rule, then, may be thus stated :—

" All dissonances must be introduced by consonances," or, in other words, " The sound which constitutes the dissonance must first be heard in the preceding chord as a consonance."

And this is called *preparing* a dissonance.

And it is also evident from this, that in whatever part (treble, bass, or inner) the dissonance occurs, in that same part it must also be prepared.

It will also be noted, that the dissonance always descends one degree upon the following consonance.

And this is called *resolving* a dissonance.

A few examples will make this clearer :—

If we wanted to introduce the dissonance of the fourth into this harmony, we might do so, perhaps, as follows :—

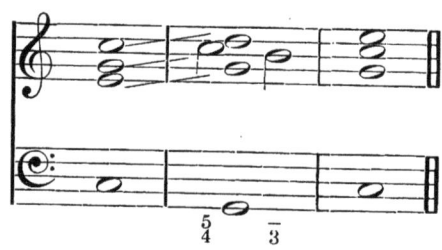

But on inspecting the progression of these parts, it will soon be seen that the fourth is *not prepared.*

To remedy this defect, it must be introduced *into the same part* in the preceding bar; thus—

And the same process would enable us to introduce the dissonance of the ninth into the last bar; thus—

And the dissonance of the sixth should be prepared and resolved in the same manner.

The following rules will be useful :—

I. The dissonance of the fourth may be introduced whenever the fundamental bass (or root) descends a fourth or ascends a fifth.

II. The dissonance of the ninth may be introduced whenever the fundamental bass ascends a fourth or descends a fifth.

The preceding example will serve to illustrate both these rules.

5. The preceding remarks refer only to dissonances by suspension occurring in *uninverted chords*. By employing inverted basses, a great variety of effects by suspension may be obtained.

In every case care must be taken "never to let the suspending note be heard together with the note it suspends." Thus

would be wrong; as the suspended B is heard in the tenor part. In a free style, however, such a combination is occasionally met with.

Still, it is necessary for the student to keep to the rule; excepting only in the case of the ninth by suspension, which *may* be used with the eighth, *provided the parts proceed by contrary motion*, and only then. Indeed, even in this allowed case, the licence should be sparingly used. Thus, for instance,

would be allowed by licence, while the following—

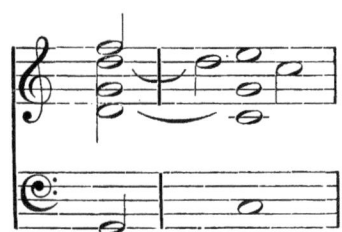

would be altogether inadmissible. For it is evident that hidden consecutive octaves would be produced—

6. In the first inversion of the common chord, the fundamental dissonance of the ninth becomes a seventh to the inverted bass, as follows :—

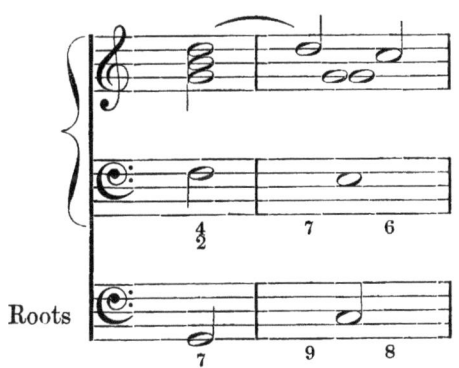

Here the leading note, B, is allowed by licence to fall to G, to avoid
the transgression of the above rule for the resolution of dissonances.

In this inversion the fundamental dissonance of the sixth becomes
a fourth to the inverted bass ; as thus—

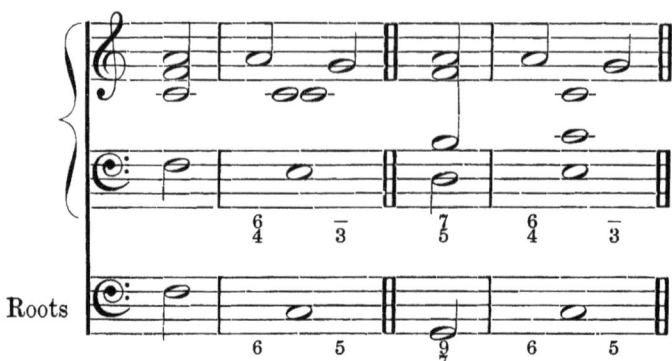

In the second case here given, the dominant seventh, F, has been allowed to fall to C instead of E, in order to avoid breaking the same rule.

In this inversion the fundamental dissonance of the fourth necessitates the suspension of the inverted bass itself; thus—

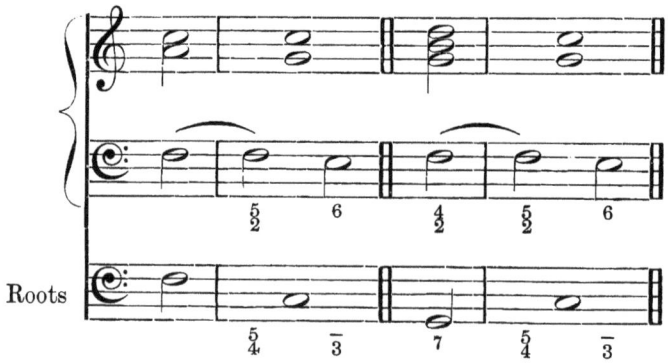

for the inverted bass is always to be looked upon as an upper melody transposed into the lowest place, and therefore to be treated in all respects as such.

In the second inversion of the common chord, the fundamental dissonance of the fourth becomes a seventh to the inverted bass, thus—

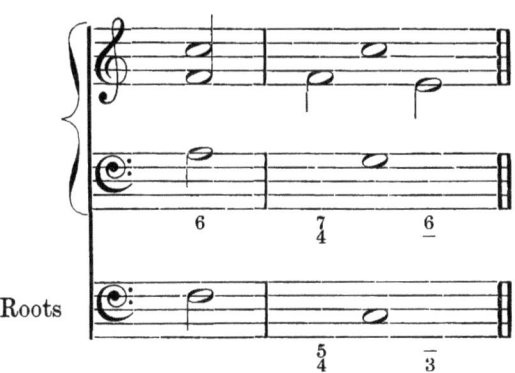

In this inversion the fundamental dissonance of the ninth becomes a fifth to the inverted bass, thus—

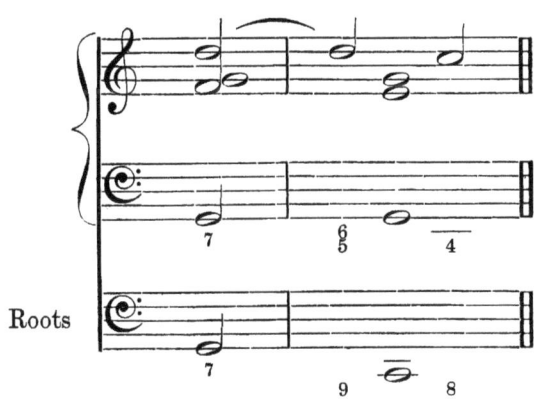

In this inversion the fundamental dissonance of the sixth involves the suspension of the inverted bass itself, producing the following :—

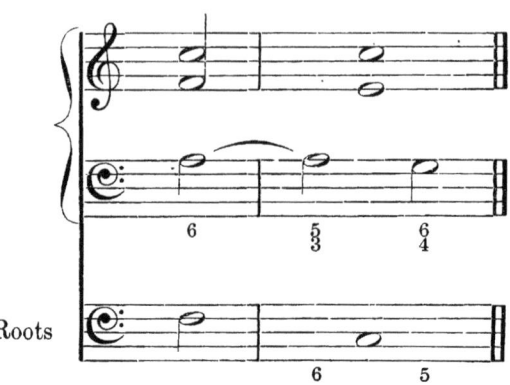

In the inversions of the chord of the dominant seventh the various dissonances will appear as follows. The student will understand them without further explanation.

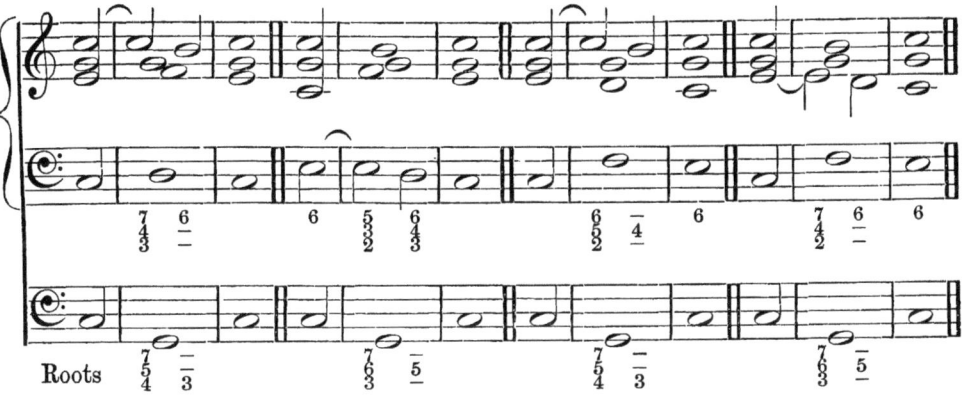

In none of these cases has the dissonance of the ninth been admitted, because it becomes identical, practically, with the chord of the added ninth, already described; or, if minor, with the chord of the minor ninth.

The student will now be able to add dissonances by suspension to the chords of the added and minor ninths and their inversions, by carefully adhering to the rules given above. We will therefore give a bass with figures, and with the roots indicated, for him to harmonize.

To render this easier, however, the following rules will be useful. The first and second have already been given in other words.

I. When the fundamental bass (or root) descends a fourth, or ascends a fifth, the dissonance of the fourth may be introduced, prepared by the octave.

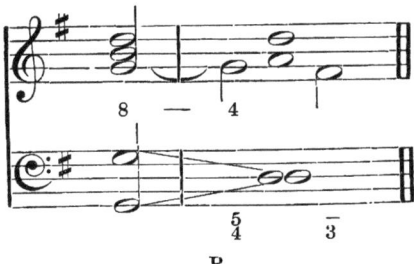

P

II. When the root ascends a fourth, or descends a fifth, the dissonance of the ninth may be introduced, prepared by the fifth.

III. When the root descends a fourth, or ascends a fifth, the dissonance of the sixth may be introduced, prepared by the third.

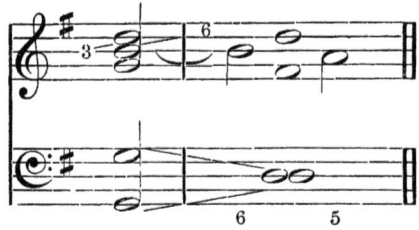

IV. When the root ascends a second, the dissonance of the ninth, prepared by the third, and that of the fourth, prepared by the fifth, may be introduced.

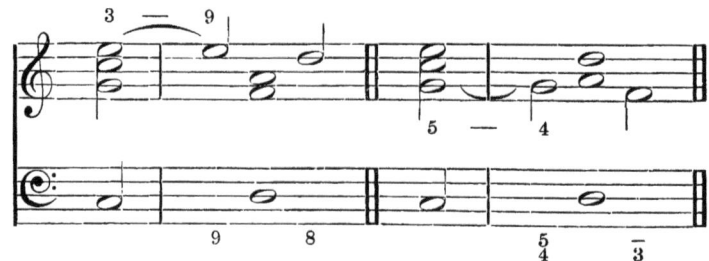

V. When the root ascends a third, the dissonance of the sixth, prepared by the third, may be introduced.

VI. When the root ascends a sixth, or descends a third, there can be no dissonance.

VII. When the root descends a second, or ascends a seventh, the dissonance of the sixth, prepared by the fifth, or that of the fourth, prepared by the third, may be introduced.

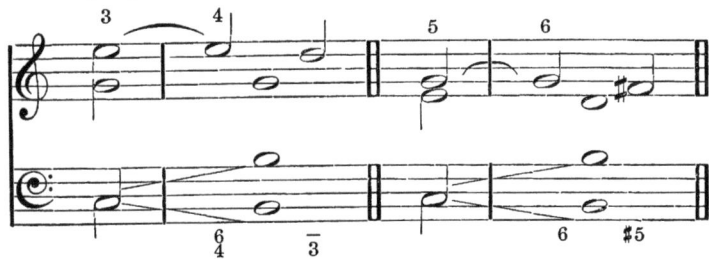

[When inverted basses are used, and dominant harmonies added, certain additional rules may be added.]

VIII. When the root of preparation bears a dominant seventh, and ascends a fourth, or descends a fifth, the dissonance of the fourth, prepared by the seventh, may be introduced.

IX. When the root of preparation bears an added ninth or a minor ninth, and ascends a fourth, or descends a fifth, the dissonance of the sixth, prepared by the ninth, may be introduced.

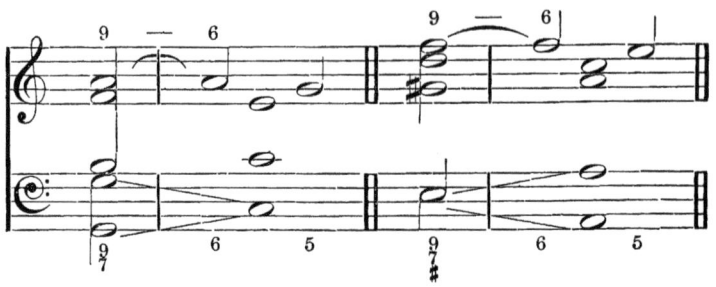

Exercise on Dissonances.

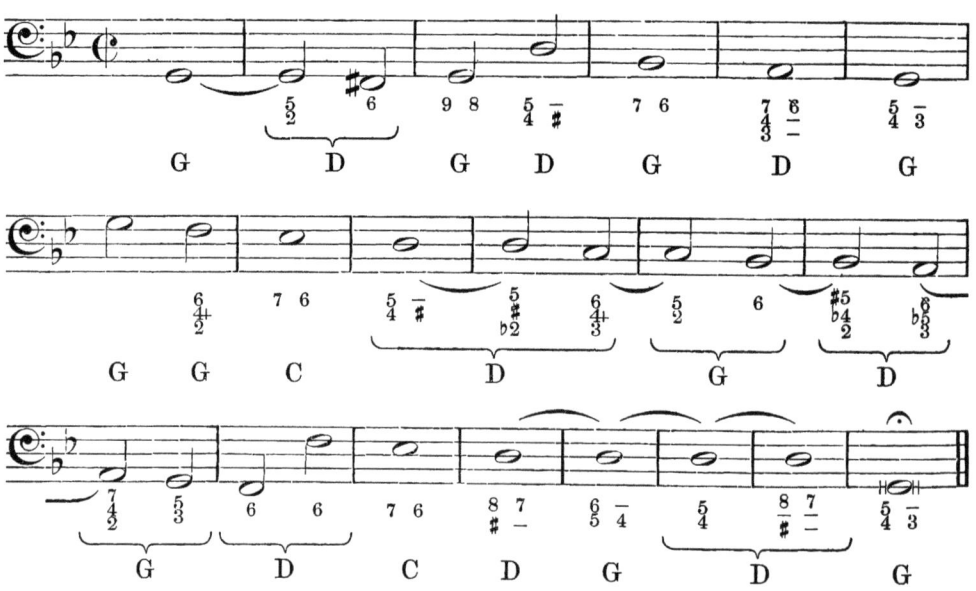

7. When two dissonances can be regularly introduced on the same root, according to the foregoing rules, they may be introduced simul-

taneously. They are then called *double dissonances*, and the chord into which they are introduced is called a *double discord*.

Thus we may have the double dissonance of the fourth and ninth. For example—

$$\begin{matrix} 6 \\ 5 \end{matrix} \qquad \begin{matrix} 9 \\ 4 \end{matrix} \qquad \begin{matrix} 8 \\ 3 \end{matrix}$$

We may likewise have the double dissonance of the sixth and fourth. For example—

$$\begin{matrix} 6 \\ 4 \end{matrix} \qquad \begin{matrix} 5 \\ 3 \end{matrix}$$

It is important to observe carefully the identity of the notes composing this last double discord with those forming the second inversion of the common chord. In nine cases out of ten, a $\begin{smallmatrix} 6 \\ 4 \end{smallmatrix}$ must be treated as a dissonance, and not as an inverted triad; i.e. the dissonant notes must be prepared and resolved according to the rules given in this Chapter.

Whenever a $\begin{smallmatrix} 6 \\ 4 \end{smallmatrix}$ is followed by a $\begin{smallmatrix} 5 \\ 3 \end{smallmatrix}$ on the same bass, we may be sure it is a dissonance, and must act accordingly. The root will then, of course, be different from what it would be, were the chord the inversion of a triad. Thus the root of the first note in this bar,

is not G, but D; and bears the double dissonance of the sixth and fourth. Therefore both the B and the G must be sounded, in the same parts, in the previous chord; thus—

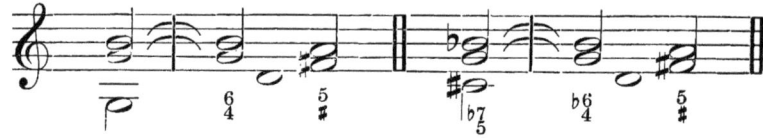

8. i. The dissonance of the ninth may be resolved on the sixth, if the bass ascends a third—

ii. The dissonance of the sixth may be resolved on the third, if the bass ascends a third—

iii. The dissonance of the sixth, may be resolved on the sixth, if the bass descends one degree—

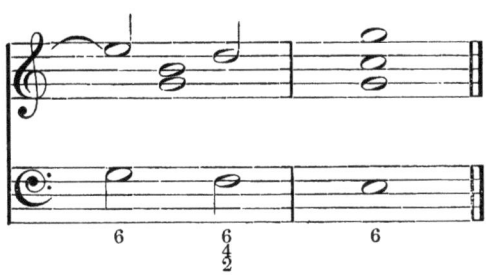

iv. The dissonance of the fourth may be resolved on the sixth, if the bass descends a fourth, or ascends a fifth—

9. It will also be useful to remember that while fundamental discords are resolved on *another bass*, discords by suspension are resolved on the *same bass*. Also it is well to bear in mind that while fundamental discords require *no preparation*, but *only resolution*, discords by suspension require both *preparation* and *resolution*.

CHAPTER IX.

1. IN Chapter VIII, section 3, it was said that "When an interval of a melody (or of an inner part) is kept back in *descending*, it is called a *suspension*.

It remains now to treat of the other case : "When an interval of a melody (or of an inner part) is kept back in *ascending*, it is called a *retardation*."

The principle of the two is the same, only that the name of *suspension* is not, strictly speaking, suitable to the case of a note *kept from ascending*.

2. When the leading note is retarded, the dissonance of the *major seventh by retardation* is produced.

This is prepared by the third, and can be introduced whenever the root falls a fifth, or rises a fourth.

When the fifth is retarded, the dissonance of the *second by retardation* is produced.

This is prepared by the fifth, and can be introduced whenever the root falls a fifth, or rises a fourth; if the fifth is so placed as to be able to rise a degree.

These are the only fundamental retardations.

The rules for their preparation and resolution are much the same as those which refer to suspensions.

3. When the two retardations are used together, a *double discord by retardation* is produced; thus—

The student will be able to work out the application of these dissonances to chords with inverted basses, by reference to the method employed in the case of suspensions.

4. Retardations and suspensions may likewise be variously combined:
of which we will now give some examples.*

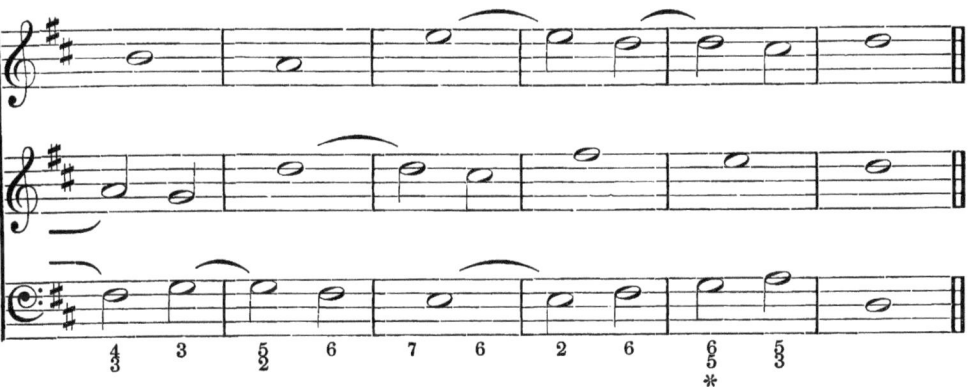

$$\begin{matrix} 4 & 3 & 5 & 6 & 7 & 6 & 2 & 6 & 6 & 5 \\ 3 & & 2 & & & & & & 5 & 3 \\ & & & & & & & & * & \end{matrix}$$

* This chord will be explained in a future Chapter.

CHAPTER X.

1. In Chapter IV, section 2, Logier's rule was quoted, that "Whenever we use a [fundamental] seventh, and thus proceed to a new key, we modulate into that key." And in the same place a regularly progressive modulation of this kind was given.

We will now give it in a more concise form.

This may be still further curtailed by the following method, whereby the octave changes to a dominant seventh in each successive chord.

But the progression can even further be shortened by omitting all the tonic triads and inversions, and regarding each successive chord of the dominant seventh, or its inversion, as embracing the proper resolution of the preceding one.

In this form the result will be as follows:—

where we may observe, 1st, that the leading notes all appear as though

they were resolved downwards, in defiance of rule.   But the ear supplies
the omitted intervening tonic chord in each case, and thus is satisfied.
Moreover, the progression of the roots, each becoming a dominant to the
next, quite overrides the effect of the irregular resolutions of the leading
notes, and carries the ear with it headlong in its downward course.   Therefore this mode of resolving leading notes is allowed, *as a licence.*   We
observe, 2ndly, that the bass and treble both proceed chromatically by
similar motion, and at the interval of a diminished fifth.   And we
observe, 3rdly, that the first and third inversions are used alternately.

Another form of this series is the fundamental position, thus—

&c., &c., &c.

Such a series is called a " sequence of dominant sevenths."

2.   Chords of the added ninth, as well as of the minor ninth, are
susceptible of similar treatment.   The latter particularly so, in the
form of diminished sevenths, thus—

&c., &c.

where, by the enharmonic substitution of G♯ for A♭ in the fourth chord we change the bass from G (which it would have been) to E, and thus confine our progression of roots to the three, E, A, and D. By similar enharmonic alterations of the intervals of any of the chords, we can of course introduce any roots we please, as was shewn in Chapter IV, section 5.

We may call this series a "sequence of minor ninths," or, if we please, a "sequence of diminished sevenths."

3. If we wish to modulate in the contrary direction, i.e. from tonic to dominant continually, our process of curtailment will not be quite so complete as that just described.

It will be well to begin our work thus—

&c., &c., &c.

This progression may be curtailed as follows—

This may be called a "reversed sequence of dominant sevenths." Also, such a phrase as—

 &c., &c.

may be called a "reversed sequence of minor ninths," or a "reversed sequence of diminished sevenths."

All these sequences necessarily involve perpetual modulation from key to key. Hereafter it will be necessary to explain another kind of sequence which never modulates out of the key at all.

It will be a good exercise, meanwhile, for the student to introduce dissonances by suspension and retardation into the various sequences we have now described, and to vary the inversions employed in as many ways as he possibly can.

4. It is now time that we should give a few general rules for the harmonizing of melodies, which will be found useful to the student. They have, for the most part, been selected from Logier.

   i. When the fifth of the dominant chord is in the melody, it is a good plan to take the third of the root in the bass, and harmonize it as a $\frac{6}{5}$.

   ii. When the third of the dominant chord is in the melody, it is best to take the seventh of the root for the bass, and harmonize it as a $\frac{6}{4}{2}$.

   iii. When the third is in the melody (whether of dominant or tonic), and the seventh cannot be taken as the bass, adopt the fundamental bass.

   N.B. These three rules may be *reversed*, i.e. the intervals of the bass and melody may change places.

   iv. When the seventh is in the melody, the fifth *may* be taken as the bass, and harmonized $\frac{6}{4}{3}$.

   v. When the fifth is in the melody, the seventh *may* be taken as the bass, and harmonized $\frac{6}{4}{2}$.

   N.B. Whenever an accidental sharp occurs in a melody, we may regard it as indicating a *modulation*, and it will usually be the leading note ascending to the new tonic. Similarly an accidental flat may be regarded in most cases as a minor seventh descending to the third of the new tonic. Hence the use of the following rules.

R

vi. A note of modulation which ascends a semitone, modulates either to the key which lies a semitone above it, whether major or minor, or to the relative minor of the above-named major key.

vii. A note of modulation which descends a semitone, modulates either to the key of which it will be the major third on so descending, or to the relative minor of that key.

viii. A note of modulation which descends a whole tone, modulates either to the key which lies a whole tone below it, or to the relative minor of that key, or to the key of the fifth below the note to which it descends.

ix. A note of modulation which ascends a whole tone, can only modulate to one key, to which it will be a major third after thus ascending.

x. When any note is repeated, it may modulate to the key of which it is the fifth.

ix. A note of modulation which ascends a fourth or descends a fifth, modulates to a key to which it will be the octave, or to a key to which it will be a fifth. In either case the modulation may lead to a major or minor key.

CHAPTER XI.

1. HITHERTO in deriving the various intervals of tonic and dominant harmony from the natural harmonics of a root, we have confined ourselves to prime numbers, except in the solitary instance of the major ninth.

This interval occurs in the third octave,* and is produced by $\frac{1}{9}$ of the length of a pipe or string, the ratio of the velocity of its vibrations being to those of the root as 9 : 1.

Compared with the harmonic No. 3 (which is the twelfth of the root or the fifth in the first octave), it is as 9 : 3, or as 3 : 1. Accordingly its pitch is the twelfth (or octave fifth) above that interval.

It is on account of that intermediate link between the major ninth and the root that it is a very pleasant interval to the ear, more so indeed than the untempered minor seventh of nature, which is a prime number, 7.

2. The fifth of the root, or dominant, has been made the basis of the whole super-structure of harmony; as has been sufficiently shewn in the preceding pages, especially in Chapter II, sections 2 and 3.

Supposing now that it were found necessary to have a second derivative root, in order to explain the formation or origin of certain fundamental discords, what harmonic of the original root would offer the best hope of a satisfactory solution?

Clearly that one which affords new secondary harmonics the least remote from the tonic root.

* See Paradigm at head of Chapter IV.

The first which would suggest itself would probably be the major third, which occurs in the second octave, and is represented by the ratio 5 : 1. But on examining the harmonics of it, we find that its perfect fifth is the same note (No. 15) as we already possess as our dominant leading note, and that the next foreign interval it gives us (i.e. its major third) is the augmented fifth of the root, or the augmented octave of the dominant ; which would be represented by the No. 25, if the paradigm in Chapter IV were carried far enough.

It is indeed possible that this interval so derived *may* occasionally be of use to account for the introduction of the *augmented triad*, for instance—

and for certain progressions and modulations to be mentioned in their place. But on the whole we may conclude that the major third of the root will not answer our purpose as a supplementary or secondary root, since its available harmonics are both few and remote.

Still less will the fundamental minor seventh answer; for not only is it still more remote, but it also produces intervals, every one of which would require the same great amount of alteration and tempering as is required in its own case.

We are therefore driven to the *major ninth*, which will be found to answer well.

It is not so remote in reality as it at first sight appears to be, because it is produced by a square number $3 \times 3 = 9$, and is therefore, as an interval, the fifth of the fifth of the root; or rather, as we should say, the dominant of the dominant.

It is therefore as intimately connected with the dominant, as the dominant is with the tonic.

Moreover, as will be shewn when we come to speak of "the tonic pedal," all the harmonics of this secondary root, even up to its minor and major ninths, will sound well when combined with the tonic and dominant roots, separately or in conjunction.

Whenever then discords of a fundamental character occur, which cannot be accounted for by referring them to a dominant root, they must be classed as derived from the major ninth of the root, which is the dominant of the dominant, and which, from its place in the diatonic scale as the second degree, is named "the supertonic."

3. But it may be asked, 'Do cases often occur which require this expedient to solve them?' To which the reply is, That they are of constant occurrence, and that it is marvellous that theorists should have gone on confusing themselves with inadequate explanations for generations past, without having recourse to so simple a method of accounting for difficulties which were continually arising.

The earliest treatise in which recourse has been had to this method of explaining certain chords (as far as the author is aware), is Day's "Treatise on Harmony," London, 1845. He only applies the principle to the "chord of the augmented sixth," but it is really susceptible of a much wider application.

However, as this is perhaps the most obvious case, let us consider it first in order.

4. If we take the second inversion of a dominant seventh, such as

and lower the bass-note a chromatic semitone by an accidental flat, thus—

we shall produce a discord which is called * a "*French sixth*" by many writers, and is very common in modern music.

* Vide *Crotch*, "Elements of Musical Composition," pp. 71, 72 (4to., London, 1812).

Again, if we take the second inversion of a dominant seventh—

omitting the octave of the root, and lower the bass note as before—

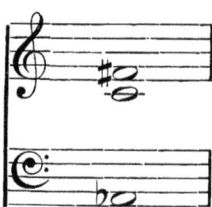

we shall produce a discord which has been called an "*Italian sixth.*" This* has been in use in Italy and elsewhere for more than 150 years.

Again, if we take the second inversion of the chord of the minor ninth, omitting the root, thus—

and then lower the bass note, as before—

---

* Logier in his " System of the Science of Music " calls this chord simply the " chord of the sharp sixth." But as the sixth is not sharp only, but *augmented*, it is better to call it, as Day does, the " chord of the augmented sixth."

we produce a discord,* which has been called by the same authorities the "*German sixth.*"

These names are very unmeaning and unsystematic; but as they are frequently employed, it is well for the student to make himself familiar with them, and with the chords they are used to denote.

5. Now it is clear that in each of these chords every note, *except the lowest which has been altered*, is derived from the root D, and belongs to that key of which D is the dominant, viz. G.

But if the chord be played several times in succession, alternately with the chord of G, thus—

the ear will be anything but satisfied, and will desire to hear the harmony of C; as thus—

* Logier calls this the "compound sharp sixth."

This is enough to excite a suspicion that G is here rather a dominant than a tonic root.

And this suspicion is strengthened by the fact that, after the chord of the augmented sixth, the ear will not tolerate the *minor* common chord of G; as thus—

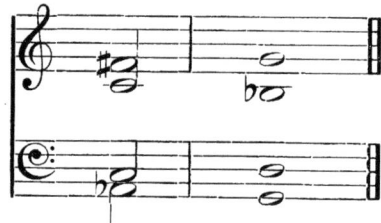

In this case, the ear imperatively calls for the *major;* thus proving that the *leading note* is required, which is the only third in the dominant harmony.

We may therefore fairly conclude that the chord of the augmented sixth must be followed by a dominant chord. Therefore its root (so far as it has been discovered hitherto by us) must be the dominant of a dominant, i.e. the *supertonic.* Therefore it belongs to the key of which it is the *supertonic,* and of which the chord into which it resolves is the *dominant.*

6. But now the question arises : What is the root of that altered bass note which could not be derived from the supertonic root ?

Clearly it is the *minor ninth of the dominant*, and being itself consequently an essentially dominant interval, it is the cause of that tendency to the real tonic which was pointed out in the last section.

7. It will be seen that the interval of the augmented sixth is formed between the minor ninth of the dominant root, and the leading note of the supertonic—

and that the only interval derived from the dominant root is its minor ninth. All the other intervals of the chord, whether it be in the forms commonly called the French, the Italian, or the German, are obviously derived from the supertonic root. Examples—

Where there are two roots, the figures of the secondary root are written above, and those of the primary root below.

8. The following rules may be found useful in resolving this discord :—*

    i. If in the resolution both notes forming the augmented sixth move, the lower one must fall, and the upper one rise a minor second, to a note which is either the octave or the fifth to the root of the next chord. Example—

    ii. If in the resolution one note only moves, while the other remains still, the moving note may approach the other by a *chromatic semitone*. Example—

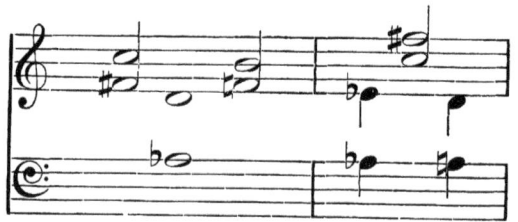

    iii. The intervals derived from the supertonic root are treated (except as restricted above) just as if it were a simple dominant, and as though the minor ninth of the other root

---

* Vide "Treatise on Harmony," by Alfred Day, M.D. (8vo., London, 1845), p. 124.

were away : provided only that they make no false progressions with that ninth.

We will now give some of the many different ways of resolving the
chord of the augmented sixth, whether accompanied by a third, a fourth,
or a fifth ; in other words, whether Italian, French, or German.

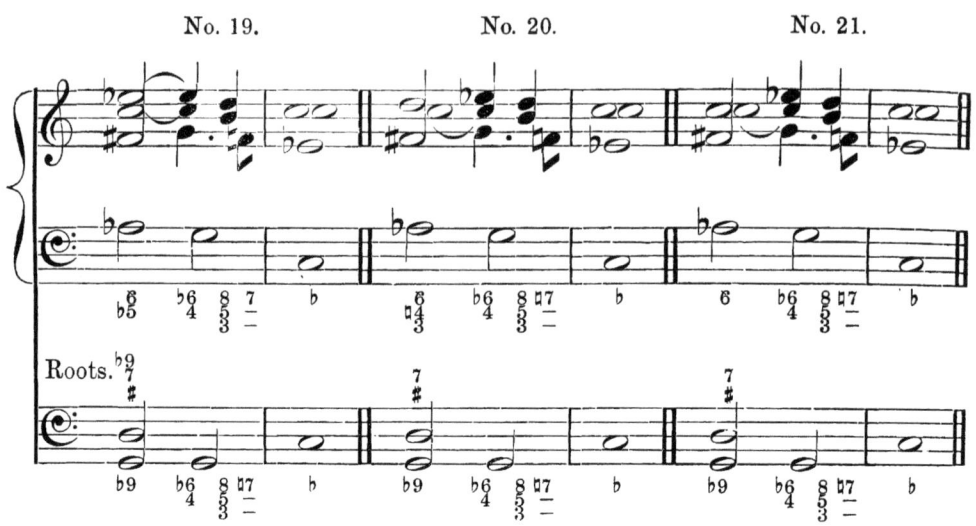

No. 31.   No. 32.   No. 33.

&c., &c., &c.

With reference to these examples, it will be well to observe that, in every one of them, the supertonic discord is first resolved, and, after that, the dominant discord.

In Nos. 3, 4, 26, and 27, the E♭ descends to C before going to its proper resolution D, in order to avoid consecutive fifths with the bass.

In Nos. 5, 8, 9, 12, 15, 18, 20, and 21, the dissonance of the sixth by suspension is not duly prepared. But it may be remarked, that the rule about preparation is often relaxed in the case of the dissonance of the sixth; especially if it have the fourth with it, and if this latter dissonance be duly prepared, which is the case here, all through.

In Nos. 22, 23, 24, 25, 26, 27, 28, 29, 30, 31, 32, and 33, the intervening octave to the dominant root is omitted, for the sake of curtailment, and the minor seventh introduced by chromatic descent of the leading note, as explained in Chapter X, section 1, shewing how a chord of the augmented sixth may form part of a regular sequence.

In Nos. 28, 29, 30, 31, 32, and 33, by the use of the fourth inversion of the chord of the minor ninth, a resolution is effected on the second inversion of the tonic triad. But this is *by no means* recommended, although it is strictly speaking allowable.

9. By the use of an enharmonic change, the augmented sixth and the minor seventh become interchangeable; by which means great variety of modulation may be obtained: for instance—

where these intervals are enharmonically substituted for each other in two places with good effect.

A particularly good instance of this way of using the enharmonic change, in treating the chord of the augmented sixth, may be found in Dr. Crotch's Oratorio of "Palestine," in the chorus "Let Sinai tell."*

* See Examples at the end of the work, Nos. 4 and 8.

T

By combining this plan with the alternate use of the chords of the diminished seventh and augmented sixth, the following curious chromatic sequence may be constructed—

&c., &c., &c.

This formula may be found useful when a sudden modulation to a remote key is required.

10. The chord of the augmented sixth can be inverted—

First Inversion.

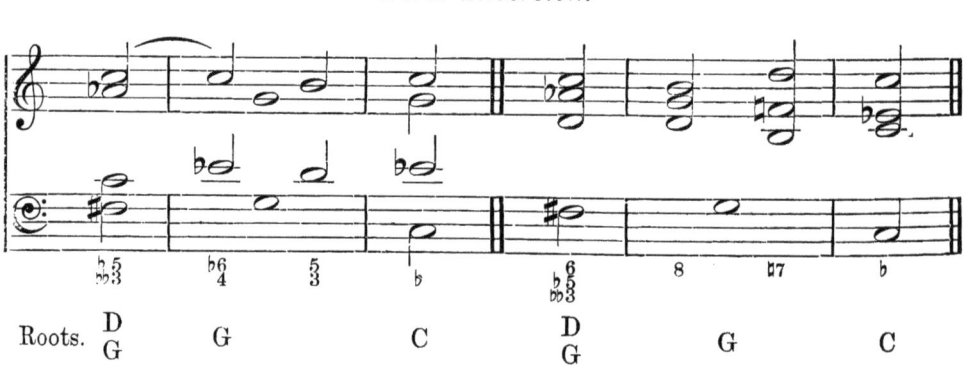

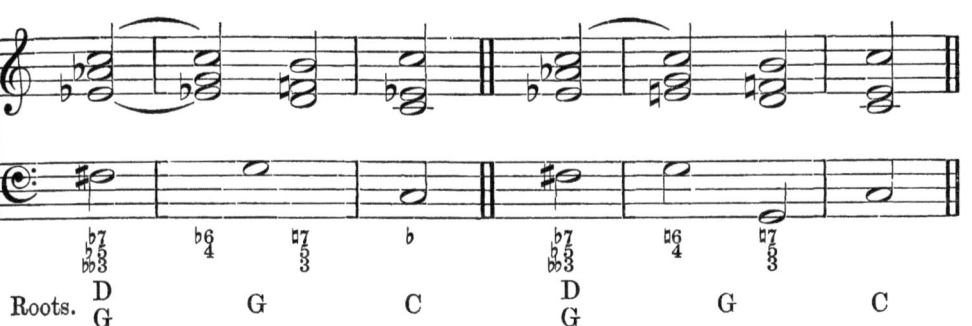

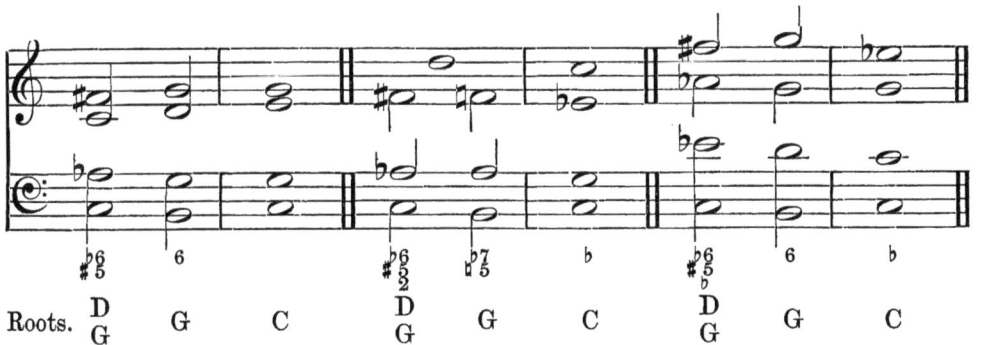

Second Inversion.

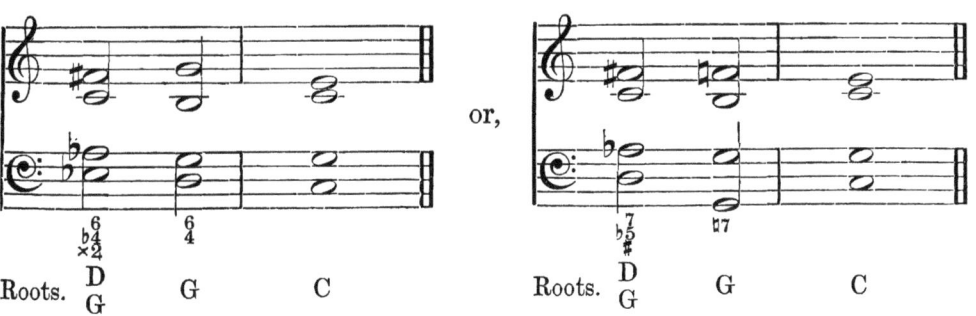

Third Inversion.

or,

T 2

NOTE.—Dr. Day denies that the interval of the augmented sixth can be inverted, on the ground that the harmonies derived from the secondary root must not be placed below those derived from the primary.

But in the first place we may imagine the roots to be distant as many octaves below as we please, so that we can always suppose the two roots to be at their proper interval apart, viz. a twelfth.

And, in the next place, the chord *has* been used in an inverted position by many of the most esteemed composers with excellent effect. The earliest instance being in Weldon's Anthem "Hear my crying," near the end of the concluding movement. (Vide Boyce's Collection of Cathedral Music, vol. ii. p. 218, of the editions of 1768 and 1788.)

Weldon was a pupil of Henry Purcell, and died in 1736.*

11. As this seems the most fitting place for explaining the meaning of what is called "false relation," or "cross relation;" it may be stated that by these terms are signified certain *harmonic incongruities* between two different parts or voices, which are exceedingly offensive, and generally forbidden.

The general rule is, that "when a note of the same name occurring in two successive chords is altered by an accidental, it must be sounded by the same part or voice, otherwise forbidden false relations will ensue." Thus—

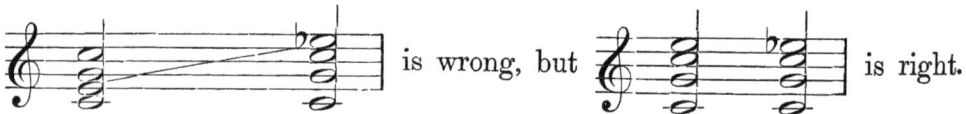

is wrong, but   is right.

The reason of which is, that the false relation gives the impression of two different keys simultaneously used; for, in the former and incorrect example here given, the treble—

* See Short Examples at the end of this work, Nos. 1 and 2.

is part of a melody in C minor, while the other parts—

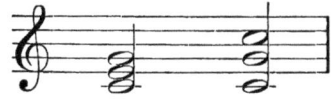

clearly belong to C major.

If, however, the note to be altered is *doubled*, it need only progress according to the above rule in one of the parts, otherwise consecutive octaves would ensue—

By licence false relations are allowed in purely dominant modulations, when occurring between different symmetrical phrases or groups; thus—

where the two phrases are enclosed in brackets, and the false relation of the G and G♯ is not harsh or unpleasant.

Where the roots proceed regularly from dominant to tonic in a descending cycle of fifths, or where such regular cycle is symmetrically reversed, false relations may sometimes be *tolerated:* for example—

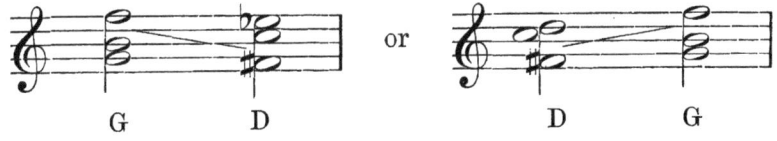

because the regular resolution of the dissonant notes in each case consoles the ear, and mitigates the harshness of the false relation.

Great composers have occasionally used considerable licence in the matter of false relations; but we do not recommend the young composer to follow their example. We have given some curious and exceptional instances at the end of this work.*

It may also be observed that in many cases the interposition of an intervening chord will not save the false relation: for instance—

In each of these cases the harsh effect of the false relation remains, because the intervening dominant chords belong equally to the major and minor mode, and therefore do not interfere with the impression produced by the two incongruous tonic chords between which they are placed.

In strict counterpoint the rules against false relations are even more exactly enforced. The above observations, however, will suffice for the student's ordinary guidance.

* See Short Examples, Nos. 16, 17.

CHAPTER XII.

1. In dealing with the chord of the augmented sixth, it was only found necessary to make use of one interval belonging to the dominant root, i.e. the minor ninth; all the rest being derived from the secondary or supertonic root.

But whenever we find a chord with a minor third and a minor seventh, we may be sure it comes from two roots.

For the minor seventh demands a *major* third, or leading note, to enable it to resolve regularly.

If we substitute a *minor* third, our root is necessarily altered. Thus—

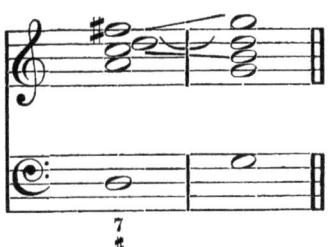

is a regular resolution of the chord of the dominant seventh of D to the tonic common chord of G.

Here, of course, the leading note F ♯ rises to the octave of the tonic, G.

But let us substitute *F natural*, and a totally different effect will be produced on the ear—

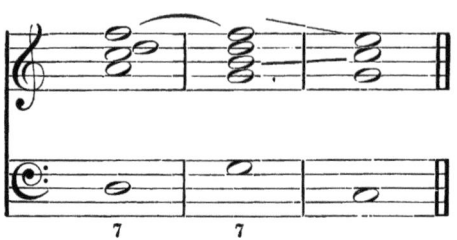

For here, evidently, we must regard the F natural as the minor seventh of the dominant root G, while the A and the C are as evidently the fifth and minor seventh of the supertonic or secondary root D.

This chord then has clearly a double root—

and the supertonic discord is resolved first, and then the dominant discord, just as was found to be the case in the chord of the augmented sixth.

2. This is a most important chord in several ways; for, in the first place, its first inversion has been known to almost all theorists and didactic writers on harmony as the "chord of the added sixth," or " great sixth "—

and they treat of it as though it were the triad of the subdominant with the arbitrary addition of this "added sixth," which is an interval entirely foreign to that root.

It is submitted that such an explanation is wholly unwarranted and unphilosophical.

For the harmonic sound No. 13 (see paradigm, Chapter IV) is clearly connected with *dominant* harmony, if with any, and is most remote from that part of the harmonic series which gives the tonic triad. Therefore, if this chord belong to the root F, it can only do so on the supposition that F is a *dominant* root, and that it belongs to the key of B flat.

But as the chord in question *does not* belong to B flat, and *does* belong to the key of C, it follows that F cannot be the root of the chord.

Nor can D be the root, as we have already shewn, because the third and seventh from such a root cannot both be minor, as they would be in this case.

C, again, cannot be the root, as the F would be a fourth, and the A a sixth—intervals which are not, strictly speaking, natural harmonics. And even supposing we regarded the F and A as represented by those very imperfect and doubtful sounds, Nos. 11 and 13 in the series of harmonics, we should still not find them to be connected with C as

U

their root, for they would then be only applicable to C if it were regarded as a dominant root; but this is not the case, for the chord does not belong to the key of F, but to that of C.

Again, Dr. Day argues at length to prove that the root is the dominant G, bearing its fifth, seventh, ninth, and eleventh.

But to this explanation there are several grave objections.

The first is that the F in this chord, especially when in the bass, has a habitual tendency to *rise*, and is quite devoid of that peculiar *downward* character which marks the dominant seventh: nor is it a sufficient answer to this objection to reply that this downward tendency is destroyed by the absence of a leading note; for an ordinary dominant seventh with the third omitted, still retains the tendency to descend very unmistakeably, as the following example will sufficiently shew—

Of course it may be said that this argument also applies to the explanation given in this section. But it should be borne in mind that we *know* the downward tendency of the fundamental seventh, and connect it in our minds with the great flatness of that interval as it appears in nature ; whereas we know that a real perfect fourth or eleventh does not exist anywhere among the harmonics, and that the interval which occupies the eleventh degree of the series, and is supposed to represent the fundamental eleventh, is so very sharp as to be much more like an *augmented* fourth or eleventh than a perfect one.

Therefore it is against the indications of nature to treat of the fundamental eleventh as though its natural tendencies could form the basis of any argument.

The next objection is the unnecessary intrusion of the *eleventh* as a fundamental harmony.

For in all cases in which this interval is supposed to exist, it may equally well be considered to be either the minor seventh of a secondary root, or a dissonance by suspension. Why then intrude it here?

3. Without going further into this matter, let it then be assumed that the " chord of the added sixth," as it is generally and erroneously called, is nothing more than the first inversion of the chord of the minor seventh with a minor third; and that it is derived from two roots, the dominant and the supertonic.

This last chord has three inversions—

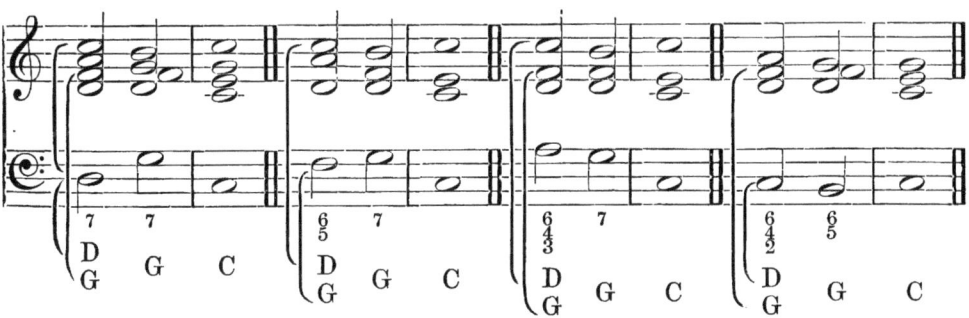

When used in the minor mode, the A, which is the ninth of the root G, becomes a *minor ninth*, A flat.

Or, taking the key of A minor, as before, for our examples, we shall have the chord and its inversions as follows—

U 2

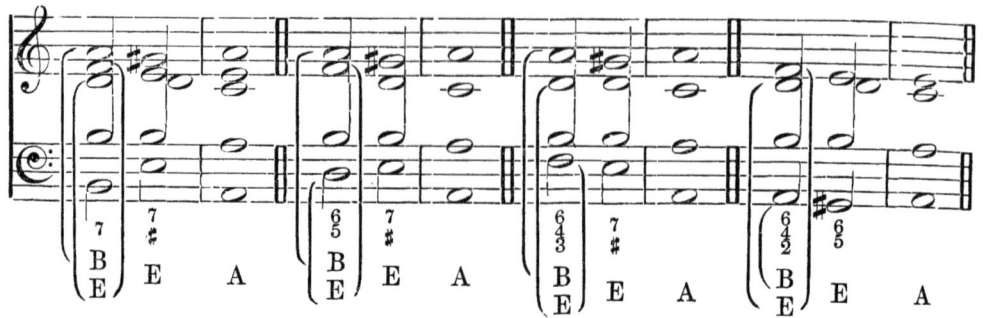

4. Sometimes, especially in modern music, the regular resolution of
the first inversion of this chord is curtailed by the omission of the
dominant chord, which usually intervenes between the double-root chord
and its final tonic resolution. This curtailment may take place either in
its major or minor variety. Thus—

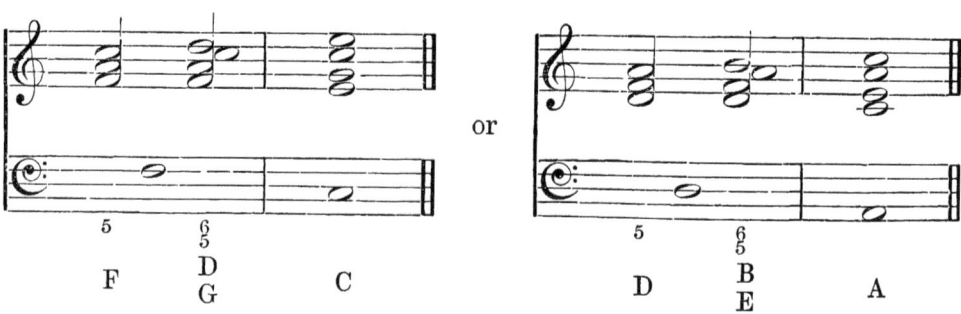

Sometimes the minor discord is followed by a major tonic triad,
after the manner of what is called a " Tierce de Picardie" (see Chapter
XIII, 3), when the following result is produced— *

* See Short Examples at the end of the work, No. 18.

And sometimes this occurs when the whole passage is in the major key, and when the preceding chord is also itself major, thus—

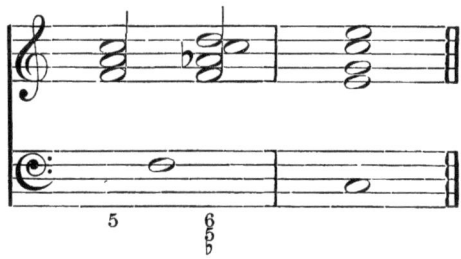

In all these cases the chord has been preceded by that of the sub-dominant; but this is far from being always the case. Moreover, the uninverted chord of the minor seventh and third, as well as its second and third inversions, may occasionally be treated after a similar manner; as will be seen by the following examples—

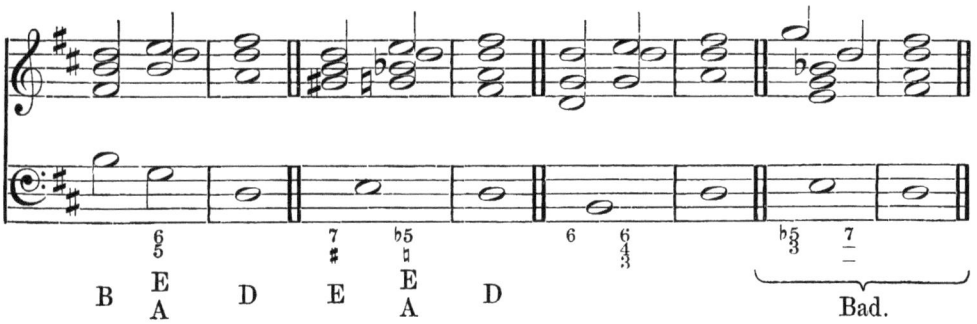

CHAPTER XIII.

Of Cadences or Closes.

1. WE are now sufficiently advanced to speak of *Cadences*, or, as they are sometimes called, *Closes*.

It is most important in a piece of music that every period, or separate clause, and especially the conclusion of the whole, should tell the ear exactly what it is intended to convey. It may be compared to ordinary speaking in this; for it is evidently essential to good speaking that the inflexions of the voice, as well as the words employed, should indicate whether any sentence be intended to be a final conclusion, or only a temporary but incomplete rest in the sense, or an exclamation, or an interrogation. So in writing, it is necessary carefully to observe correct punctuation for the same reason : the sense will often depend in a considerable degree on the right use of the various stops, the comma, the semicolon, the colon, the full stop, and the symbols of exclamation and interrogation. In music the same sort of result depends on the right use of *Cadences ;* and they are accordingly various in kind, and in their application.

2. The perfect cadence, or full close, is composed of a dominant triad, or a chord of the dominant seventh succeeded by a regular

resolution into the tonic common chord, which last should always be placed on the strong place or "down-beat" of the measure. Example—

It is still considered a perfect cadence, even when dissonances and retardations are introduced into the chord; although they somewhat weaken its effect, in most cases. Example—

The perfect cadence corresponds exactly to a full stop in writing, and should be employed whenever any portion of a piece of music is brought to its completion, and perfect rest is therefore called for.

3. If the piece is serious and solemn, and it is desirable to intensify the effect of the final perfect cadence, it is usual, especially in sacred pieces, to add to it a *plagal cadence*.

This cadence is composed of the major or minor triad of the sub-dominant, followed by the major triad of the tonic. Example—

Both triads, properly speaking, should be introduced on the down-beat of the measure.

It is often allowable and desirable to modulate regularly into the key of the subdominant, so as to introduce the plagal cadence; and here also dissonances are, admissible on the final bass-note. Example—

where the first four notes contain a perfect cadence in A minor; after which follows a regular modulation into the key of the subdominant D minor, including the dissonance of the ninth by suspension, and thus forming a regular plagal cadence to the final chord of A major.

When the major third is thus introduced into the final chord of a piece in a minor key, it is called the "Tierce de Picardie," from the district in which it is *said* to have been first used in this manner.

The plagal cadence may be used also without a previous perfect cadence, *provided the impression of the key in which the piece is to conclude is sufficiently strong on the ear.*

x

This precaution is requisite, to avoid a craving after the key of the subdominant after the piece is concluded, which is certain to ensue if the final chord partake in the least of a dominant character.

It is allowable to substitute inversions of the subdominant triad for its fundamental position, if convenient. Example—

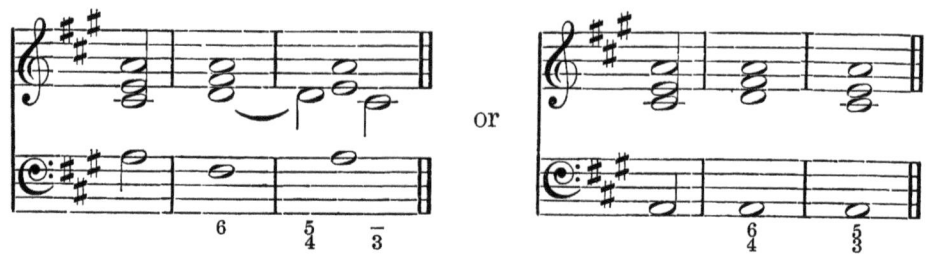

or

But the effect of this ending is not quite satisfactory to the ear. It should, therefore, be used with discretion.

4. When it is wished to make a kind of rest or division in a piece of music, so as to lead the ear to desire a resumption of the movement, after, as it were, taking breath, it is usual to employ what is called the *Imperfect Cadence*, or *half-close*.

This is the reverse of the perfect cadence, and consists of the major common chord of the dominant, preceded by the major or minor common chord of the tonic, either plain, thus—

or varied by dissonances by suspension—

or by inversions of the tonic chord, thus—

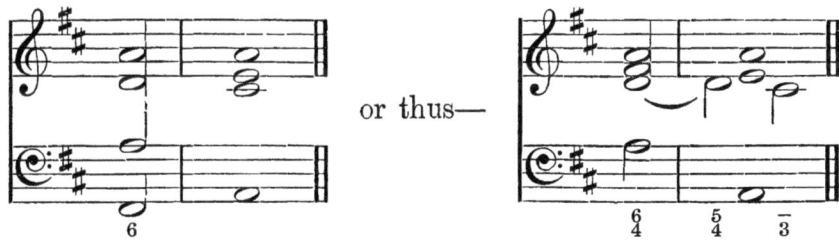

or thus—

When a melody is regularly divided into two parts by a double
bar, it is very usual to let the former part end with an imperfect
cadence, and the latter part with a perfect one. As an example of
this we will quote a well-known single chant—

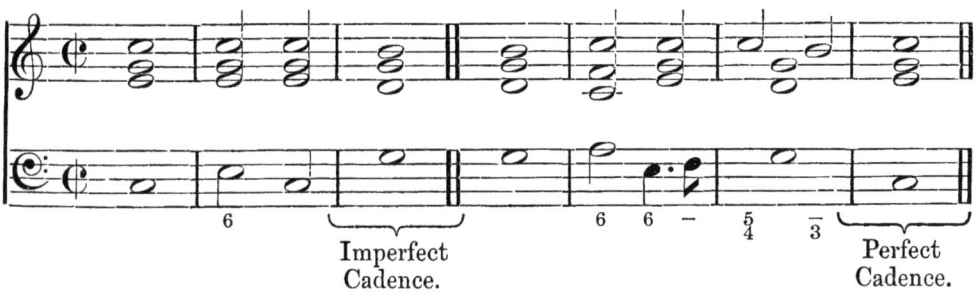

These three are the only regular kinds of cadence or close,—the
perfect, the imperfect, and the plagal.

x 2

5. The following passage from Logier * will clearly explain how to introduce a perfect cadence.

"When the chord of the fundamental seventh, or dominant harmony, proceeds *direct* to the tonic, it is called a 'perfect cadence,' as at (*a*) in the following example—

"It must have been observed, that by a continued modulation from key to key, we are kept in a state of constant excitement, approaching even to a painful sensation, so that the ear becomes desirous of rest. Therefore, when we have modulated for some time, it becomes necessary either to return to the key from which we set out, and there conclude; or, if we wish to proceed still further, first to make a close in the key at which we have arrived, and, after modulating for some time longer, to come at last to a final close.

"We must not, however, stop upon any tonic at which we may have arrived [as at (*b*) in the above example]; for, as the great object of a cadence is to lead the ear to a quiet state, an abrupt termination must destroy the effect intended. It might be supposed that the perfect cadence, described above, would be sufficient for this purpose, yet we find that this is really not the case. It is true that proceeding

* "System of the Science of Music," p. 82.

direct by the chord of the fundamental seventh to its tonic forms a perfect cadence, with which the ear would be sufficiently satisfied, where
modulations have not recently occurred [as at (c) in the above example];
yet the frequency of its occurrence in a course of modulation, although
it may not destroy, materially weakens the decisive and concluding
effect it would naturally produce under other circumstances. Therefore,
when we arrive at the tonic of any key to which we have modulated,
and desire to come to a decided and satisfactory close, the ear must
be gradually soothed into a quiescent state by the introduction of a few
chords, so constructed that they shall not only have a tendency to con-
duct the ear to a state of rest, but shall also be calculated to produce
a strong impression of the key in which it is intended the close shall
take place.

"The chords best calculated for this purpose are those of the subdominant and dominant; for the intervals of these chords (including
also those of the tonic) embrace the whole of the diatonic scale: so that,
in fact, by hearing those three chords at the close of a modulation,
we receive an 'impression of every interval of the key in which we
thus conclude. See (d) in the following example—

"However, a frequent recurrence of the simple chords of which this
cadence is constructed, would produce a heavy and rather monotonous

effect, which is much relieved by the introduction of the dissonance of the fourth upon the dominant, as at (e).

"On account of the frequent occurrence of the final cadence, composers have been induced to seek for every possible variety, and great liberties have been taken for this purpose. The fourth, as it appeared in the last example, at (e), was properly prepared; but a sixth is also sometimes introduced, which, it will be perceived, cannot be prepared, and must be considered as a licence, as at (f)."

But that is not all.

Still further to secure variety, the double-root chord of the minor seventh and minor third, especially its first inversion (which Logier calls the chord of the added sixth), is often substituted for the chord of the subdominant. And it should be borne in mind that in employing this chord the *seventh of the secondary root should be prepared as if it were a dissonance of suspension.*

Sometimes the supertonic seventh is altogether omitted, and then two curious results follow: first, we get a chord exactly like the first inversion of the minor triad of the supertonic; but in reality it is only a dominant chord of the added ninth in its third inversion: and secondly we avail ourselves of the licence, peculiar to this form of the cadence, to introduce without preparation not only the dissonance of the sixth, but also that of the fourth.

Examples—

Roots.
C G G C

&c., &c., &c.

NOTE.—It occurs frequently that a common chord, the bass of which is a third below the tonic of our key, is interpolated between the tonic and subdominant (or substituted chord). If we are in a minor key, this chord will be a major chord. If we are in a major key, the contrary will be the case. Examples—

6. In order still further to avoid monotony, other modifications and curtailments are sometimes introduced :

i. The subdominant or other substituted chord is *omitted*, the $\frac{6}{4}$ or $\frac{5}{4}$ being retained upon the dominant, thus—

ii. Or the subdominant or substituted chord retained, while the dominant $\frac{6}{4}$ or $\frac{5}{4}$ is omitted, thus—

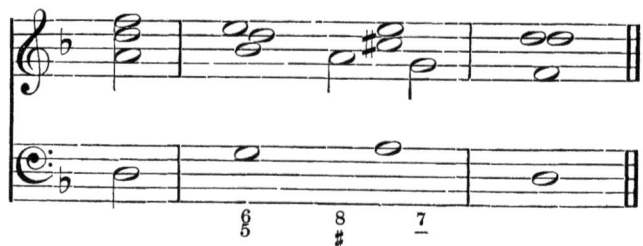

iii. The same, omitting the seventh of the supertonic, thus—

iv. Introducing the chord of the dominant seventh on the supertonic root, thus—

v. Introducing the first inversion of the same chord—

vi. Introducing the second inversion of the same chord—

vii. Or the chord of the minor ninth on the supertonic root—

Y

viii. Or the first inversion of the same chord—

ix. Or the second inversion of the same chord—

x. Or the chord of the augmented sixth—

xi. Or the inversion of the same chord—

xii. Or, lastly, a new chord, which shall be explained in the following section—

7. On comparing our new chord in No. xii. with that in No. iii.,
it will be seen that the only difference is the accidental depression of
one interval, viz. the fifth of the dominant root G.

But this interval so depressed forms no part of the harmonic
series of G.

All the rest of the chord, however, belongs to it.

From what root then is this obtruded D♭ to be derived?

Clearly from C, of which it is the minor ninth.

But judging by the analogy of the double root-chords explained
above, one might think that such a derivation of the chord from
the two roots $\frac{G}{C}$ would lead us to consider it as belonging rather to
the key of F, of which those roots are respectively the dominant and
supertonic.

And to a certain extent this is true; and thus we see a connection
between this cadence and the plagal cadence, where a transient modulation into the key of the subdominant actually takes place.

This new chord is then originally, though remotely, a subdominant
chord, though actually built on the tonic and dominant; and whatever

elements of modulation it may possess are neutralized by the essentially dominant character of the rest of the cadence.

Such then is the analysis of this remarkable and very beautiful chord.

It is peculiarly suited to the minor mode, although occasionally it may be followed by a major conclusion.

To distinguish it, it will be advisable to call it the " pathetic cadence": a name given to it by some authors on account of its peculiar character. Dr. Crotch, Callcott, and most English theorists, have named it the " *Neapolitan sixth*," but such a name is very unmeaning, as it certainly was at no time peculiar to the Neapolitan composers.

It is susceptible of two inversions; but they are difficult to manipulate, and of doubtful advantage. Therefore they may be passed over in this place.

CHAPTER XIV.

1. CADENCES which lead *from* the key, may be fitly termed "cadences of modulation." Of these there are many kinds.

   a. Irregular Cadences, or perfect cadences out of the key, designed not for final closes, but for variety. Examples—

From C to A minor.

From F minor to A flat.

From D minor to A minor.

β. *Incomplete Cadences*, which close not on the tonic triad, but on its first inversion, introduced by the third inversion of the preceding dominant chord, thus—

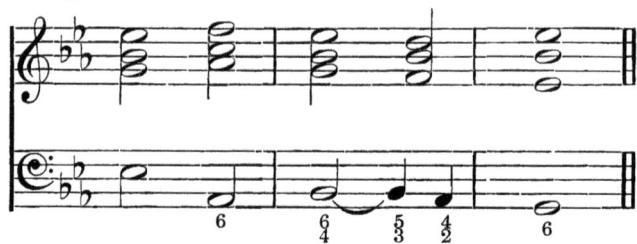

γ. *False Cadences*, where the cadence, after proceeding regularly as far as the chord of the dominant seventh, is suddenly broken in upon by the intrusion of a foreign chord; which must, however, be such as to allow all the intervals of the preceding chord to be regularly resolved, thus—

In No. i. the dominant bass, instead of descending to the tonic, rises a whole tone.

In No. ii. the same progression is accompanied by dissonances by suspension.

In No. iii. the dominant bass rises a semitone.

In No. iv. the same is shewn in the minor key. And it must be observed here that in the minor key the bass can only rise a semitone, *never* a whole tone; as, if it did, the intruded chord would produce too violent a transition for the ear to bear.

In No. v. the same in another minor key, but in a different position, and succeeding a pathetic cadence.

In No. vi. the intermediate notes are entirely omitted, making the progression short and sudden.

It is evident that no real modulation is effected in any of these cases. They are merely false cadences disappointing the ear, and requiring a subsequent cadence to restore a feeling of rest.

If then we really wish to remain in the key to which the false cadence has led us, we must make a regular cadence in that key for the purpose, thus—

And it will be seen that, by combining these two examples, we can modulate from key to key, as far as we please—

In the foregoing example (bar 5) an enharmonic substitution of B♮ for C♭ has been employed, to avoid extreme keys; at bar 7 we return to our original key. And at the end of the example a plagal cadence with dissonances has been added, in order to shew the use of such cadences to intensify the force of a perfect cadence, and to induce a feeling of final repose in the tonic.

If, however, we do not wish to modulate after the false cadence, we can always return to the original key by means of the chords of either the augmented sixth, the diminished seventh, or the seventh on the supertonic; thus—

Of course other inversions may be used, and dissonances introduced, wherever it can be done without violating any of the preceding rules.

δ. *Interrupted, or Broken Cadence.* Where a *rest* is placed where the tonic should be ; as in the following example from Logier (p. 214)—

ε. *Irregular False Cadence.* Where the chord of the dominant seventh, instead of being resolved regularly into its tonic, passes into another fundamental discord, all its intervals, however, being regularly resolved. In this case the bass descends a semitone, and the root of the new discord is the supertonic; thus—

or with any other inversion of the minor ninth, or of the chord of the dominant seventh, on D.

The chord of the added ninth may also be similarly employed.

ζ. *Suspended Cadence.* Where, instead of allowing the dominant to proceed at once to its resolution, a few modulations are interposed; thus—

CHAPTER XV.

1. IT has been already shewn (Chapter VI, sect. 3, and Chapter XI, sect. 9) how wide a field of varied modulation is opened to the composer by the equivocal character of the chord of the diminished seventh and its inversions, as well as of the chord of the augmented sixth, when these are treated enharmonically. Also it was shewn, in Chapter X, section 1, how to modulate progressively, or by way of sequence, by means of the chord of the dominant seventh and its inversions.

As a supplement to these observations it will be well to point out three other irregular or deceptive ways of modulating by means of this last-named chord, which are often of great service to the composer.

2. The minor seventh in the dominant chord, instead of descending, may ascend chromatically to a note of its own name, provided it thus becomes a leading note, and ascends afterwards to a new tonic, thus—

or it may be followed by a false cadence, thus, in the case of this
example, modulating to E minor, or to E flat major. Only provided
always that the progression of the leading note be as in the example.
Either of these chords of the seventh may be used in any of their
inversions, if the above condition be strictly observed. The leading
note of the first chord here is allowed to descend.

3. Another variety of resolution takes place when the chord of the
dominant seventh is succeeded by the first inversion of the dominant
seventh of a root a minor third below its own root—

For the second of these chords a diminished seventh on the G♯, arising
from the same root E, may be substituted.

4. The third irregular resolution of this chord is when the interval
of the minor seventh falls to the fifth of the next root, while the
leading note ascends a whole tone instead of a semitone. It is usually
confined to the first inversion of the chord, as in the annexed example—

5. Hitherto every device we have examined has had for its object the attainment of variety in modulation. But very often there may be a transition or progression from one key to another, either for a chord or two, or permanently, without any modulation properly so called. In such cases dominant harmony must be altogether laid aside, and the progress must be from one tonic triad to another. All that is wanted for this is *some note in common* between two adjoining chords, in the same part, as in the following example—

This example has been simply constructed by taking the ascending scale as a treble melody, and harmonizing each note with the three triads of which it formed a part : treating it alternately as an octave, a third, and a fifth.

It is obvious that every note is susceptible of three such harmonies, and that only such of them really belong to the *natural* scale, as coincide with the chords found for it in Chapter IV. Those which consist of the imperfect or diminished triad are ambiguous and comparatively useless. Still they have their place, and are therefore reckoned here with the rest.

6. The first note of the scale is most naturally accompanied by its lower octave, or tonic, as a bass, with its proper triad, major or minor. It may also have the subdominant for its bass, of which it is the fifth; as for instance in a plagal cadence, when that note is in the treble—

But we may also take the *third below* (either major, if we are in a minor key, or minor, if we are in a major key), and thus get a new bass, or, as it is called, a *modified* bass, which in the key of C would be A ♮ or A♭—

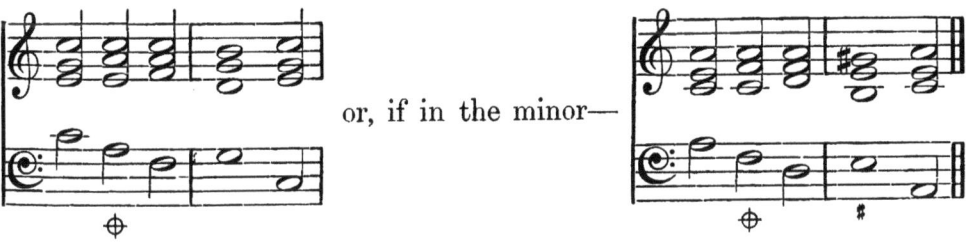

or, if in the minor—

which gives variety without modulation.

7. The second of the scale has only one natural bass, namely, the dominant, of which it is the fifth. There are, however, the two following modified basses—

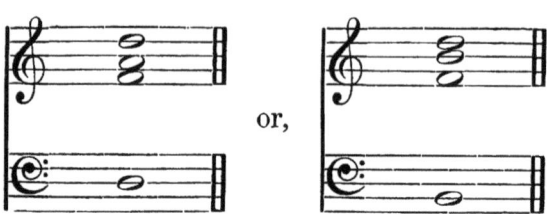

or,

Of these the former, i.e. the octave, is good; while the latter, the third below, is to be avoided, because of the diminished fifth it contains, which is a doubtful and unsatisfactory interval, suggesting the first inversion of the chord of the dominant seventh, but without the octave of the root; or else it might be an imperfect chord of the minor ninth on the third of the scale, omitting both the root and the leading note, and thus being vague, equivocal, and unsatisfactory to the ear.

8. The third of the scale has only one natural bass, which is the tonic itself. But it may be accompanied by two modified basses, i.e. one a fifth, and the other an octave below it, of which the former is to be preferred, being the relative minor—

9. The fourth of the scale has only one natural bass, namely, the sub-dominant, of which it is the octave. It may, however, be accompanied by two modified basses; one a third, and the other a diminished fifth below it. The last is of course undesirable, being the leading note, and bearing the imperfect triad—

10. The fifth of the scale has two natural basses, the tonic and the dominant. It may also be accompanied by one modified bass, the third below—

11. The sixth of the scale is naturally accompanied by the sub-dominant. It has two available modified basses, which are the fifth and the octave below—

12. The seventh of the scale has only one natural bass; it has consequently two available modified basses. But one of them should be used with caution, as it is the seventh or leading note, and bears the imperfect triad—

A a

13. The following example will shew the use of these modified basses, to secure variety, and to save continual change of key at the same time—

Here no fundamental discords, nor suspensions, nor retardations have been used, yet sufficient variety has been secured solely by the use of modified basses.

CHAPTER XVI.

1. I⊤ has already been explained how to produce sequences of various kinds.* In each case the result was a perpetual modulation round and round a cycle of keys. Now as it is obvious that such modulation, unless sparingly employed, must become very wearisome to the ear, it is desirable to find some way of combining the advantages of a regular sequence with the power of remaining in one key. And this can be done by treating dominant sevenths and ninths in a manner somewhat analogous to that by which the modified basses and triads were obtained.

2. If a chord of the dominant seventh—

be only *partially* resolved, that is to say, if the seventh fall while the leading note is suspended, the result will be as follows—

---

* See Chapter VI, section 3, and Chapter XI, section 9, and Chapter XV, section 2.

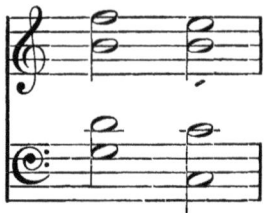

where the ear remains unsatisfied, and craves some further resolution.
This can be obtained by allowing the B to fall, as though it were the
dissonance of the ninth on the root A, in its first inversion; thus—

where we see that it is a sort of false cadence, and that the B is
really the dissonance of the ninth by suspension.

But suppose that, with a view to establish a regular progression
of the basses from fifth to fifth, we change the bass from C to F, at
the same moment that the B descends to A, we shall then introduce
another dissonance—

and this may be regarded as the dissonance of the ninth on the root D, necessitating the descent of the dissonant note E to D—

In order, however, to keep up the progression of basses as before, it will be necessary to let the basses change to B at the same time, thus producing a new dissonance of the ninth on the root G, each dissonance being in the first inversion. But instead of resolving this by allowing the A to descend to G on the same bass, we change the bass to E, thus turning the note D into a dissonance, and once more necessitating its descent to C.

Without analyzing this process further, we will give the whole sequence, and afterwards remark on some of its chords—

3. Now it will be observed that in this last example the tenor, or third part, has been varied, so as to lack the symmetry of the other parts. This has been done to avoid the hidden octaves which appear in the previous short example between the bass and tenor in each bar.

Indeed such a sequence of sevenths as this is most perfect and pure when the tenor is omitted, and when the harmony is consequently in three parts.

We will now give the same sequence in three-part harmony, and then assign the proper roots to each chord—

G   A   D   G   C   F   D/G   G   A   D   G   C   F   D/G   G   C

Here it will be perceived that the roots proceed regularly from A to F, when an interruption occurs, in the shape of a double-root chord, succeeded by an ordinary dominant seventh on G.

The chords marked * *might* have been treated as first inversions of the triad of B flat, with the dissonance of the ninth, C; but then we should have been forced to modulate out of the key, which would have destroyed the symmetry and character of our sequence.

It was preferable therefore to look on these chords as double-root chords of the minor seventh and minor third (commonly called the " seventh on the second degree "), leading back to the same dominant harmony with which we started, and with which the sequence afterwards closes.

4. By adding notes a third above the treble of the above sequence of sevenths, the *second* chord of every bar is converted into a chord of the ninth—

Again, by taking the original sequence of sevenths, and adding a tenor part progressing in sixths below the alto or second part, the *first* chord of every bar is converted into a chord of the ninth—

Or again, by combining these two sequences, a complete sequence of ninths and sevenths in five-part harmony is produced—

5. By using the inversions of the chord of the dominant seventh,
a great variety of sequences can be obtained—

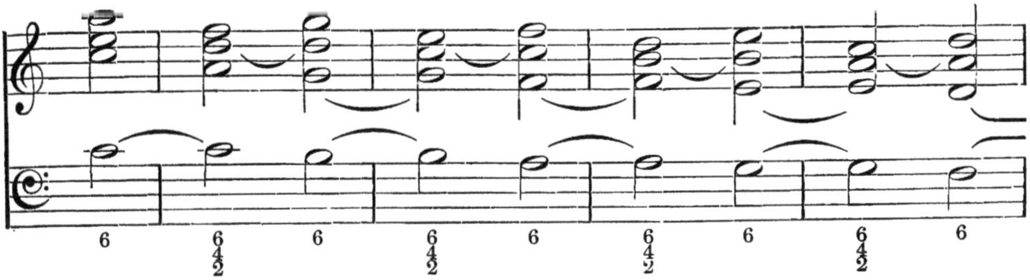

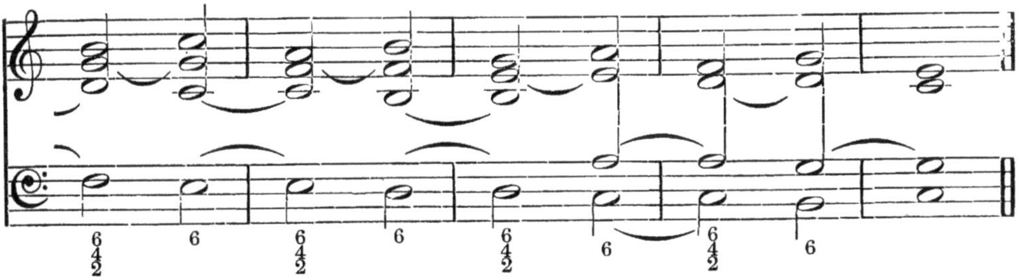

* N.B. This is not very good, as it contains hidden eights.

&c., &c., &c.

From these specimens the student will see his way to the elaboration of other forms of sequence according to the method here indicated.

The *last seventh* must be a real chord of the dominant seventh, either in its fundamental position, or inverted, so as to lead to the close on the tonic. All the other sevenths which occur in sequence are of course different from the fundamental seventh, and only derive their force from the dissonances of suspension from which they arise; and from the symmetrical progression of the basses, which gives an impulse as it were to the whole sequence, and invests it all through with a quasi dominant character. Of course it is possible to substitute a real dominant seventh at any stage of a sequence, and thus modulate into any key which that seventh leads to. This is a very useful way of availing oneself of these sequences in the course of a piece.

The annexed example is intended as an exercise for the student to harmonize—

6. Towards the close of this example occur a series of ascending notes, each figured 7 6. It will be well to say a few words about these.

Of course the simplest way of preparing these dissonances is—

which produces an ascending sequence. But this leads to the consideration of what this would be without the dissonances.

It would then become an ascending sequence of sixths accompanied by thirds; thus—

And these may either be derived from the tonic and dominant roots, or from modified basses, such as were described in the last Chapter.

B b 2

Or the same may be written in a *descending* sequence—

And this descending sequence of sixths admits of course of dissonances to each note—

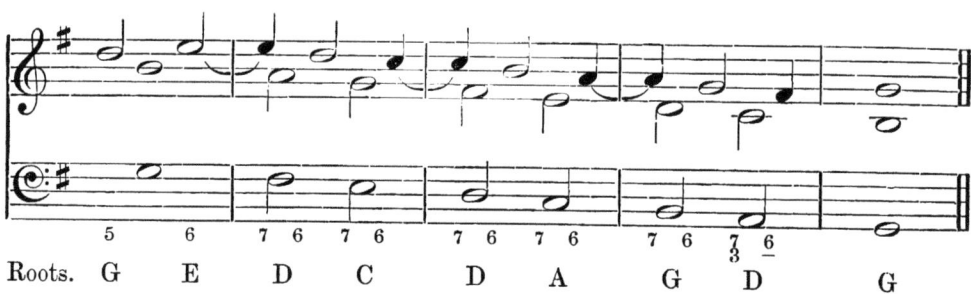

There is always considerable risk and difficulty in adding a fourth part in harmonizing a sequence of sixths, as there is danger of making hidden consecutive octaves or fifths.

The following are some of the best methods of doing it—

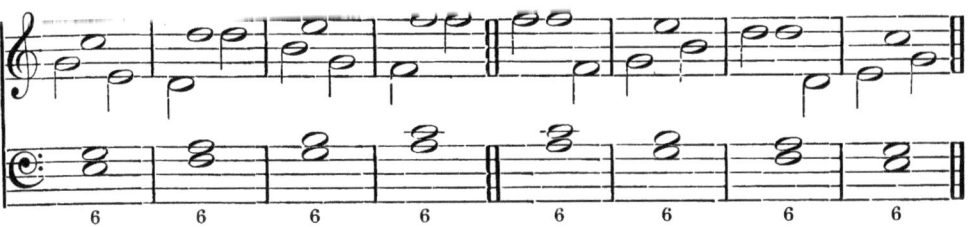

The sixths may always alternate with fifths, provided the fifths do not produce the effect of *consecutives*, which they must do, more or less, if they are on the accented beat, or (as it is called) the down-beat—

Not so good.   *Good.*

This sequence of fifths and sixths, however, is not easily practicable in descending—

The hidden fifths are here too offensive.

CHAPTER XVII.

1. WHEN the tonic or dominant root is sounded and held on, while harmonies belonging to the supertonic, dominant, tonic, and subdominant, are made use of in the upper parts, it is called a " pedal," or, as the French say, " le point d'Orgue." Any of the above harmonies may be freely used on a pedal, and many cases occur where this resource enables a composer easily to introduce discords which otherwise would seem crude and harsh.

The dominant pedal is generally introduced whenever it is wished to excite a special craving for the tonic of the original key of a piece of music, after protracted modulations; or towards the close of a fugue, for the same purpose.

The tonic pedal is only used by way of protracting the final cadence, introducing the plagal cadence gradually, or intensifying the concluding feeling of repose in the main key.

2. The way to use a pedal can be best explained by example, and a specimen is therefore given; of course it is supposed to come not near the commencement, but towards the end of a piece in the key of C. It is introduced by a few prefatory chords, and succeeded by a regular conclusion in the key of the piece—

Dissonances and sequences may be introduced freely on a pedal bass, to vary the effect.*

NOTE.— Many persons prefer neglecting the pedal altogether in the thorough-bass figuring, and placing the figures under the next lowest part, just as they would if no pedal were there. Either plan is good. If the pedal passage in this example were so figured, it would appear as follows :—

&c., &c., &c.

3. Sometimes, though rarely, a long note like a pedal is introduced in an upper or inner part of the harmony. It is necessary in that case to be very careful not to let it clash with dissonances *which resolve upon it*, especially fundamental ninths, major and minor. It is very rarely that an inner or upper part will bear this treatment, though many instances may be quoted, from the works of some of the greatest masters, where such a contrivance produces a surprisingly good effect. The proper name for it is an " Inverted Pedal."

* See Examples at the end of the work. Nos. 3, 5, 9, 10, 11.

CHAPTER XVIII.

1. A HARMONY is said to be "broken," when the intervals of which it consists are not heard simultaneously, but successively, yet so as to produce on the ear the same harmonic effect as though they were sounded together. Thus the following chords are shewn first unbroken, and then broken in various ways—

When chords are broken, care must be taken, first, that every note requiring any fixed progression or resolution, shall proceed correctly, and be resolved according to rule; and secondly, that no consecutive fifths or octaves arise in consequence of the new forms taken by the chords when broken.

2. Before going further, it may be mentioned that when a whole phrase or passage is played simultaneously in two or more different octaves, such octaves are not regarded as faulty consecutions, but the part so reinforced is said to be "doubled in octaves." Any number of

real parts may be so doubled in octaves, provided always that no consecutive fifths ensue—

This last example (iii.) however must be regarded as faulty, on
account of the consecutive fifths between the second and third parts of
the harmony. At the same time, it must be admitted that Beethoven
has made use of just such a consecution as this in the first movement

of his "Sonata for Pianoforte and Violoncello, or Horn, in F" (Op. 17), as well as in one or two other places.

Thus any of these doublings in octaves would be allowed, especially in instrumental music. And still more would it be correct to double the bass in octaves, which indeed is almost universally done in pianoforte and organ music, and in that for a full orchestra.

3. The permission to double in octaves will account for the *apparent* consecutives in the example of broken harmony given above, in the last two bars especially. And it is just in such cases as this that the student has the greatest need of care and discretion, so as to know when and how to avail himself of this resource without infringing the rules of counterpoint.

Above all he should remember that consecutive fifths can *never* be excused under plea of "doubling," although consecutive octaves can. He should also remember that the whole phrase, and not one or two notes of it, must be doubled in octaves; otherwise the rule against consecutive octaves will still be infringed upon.

4. From the consideration of broken chords the transition is easy to that of what are called "passing notes."

These "passing notes" should be regarded as nothing more than embellishments, and as in no respect affecting the harmony.

They form no part of the essential chords belonging to the melody, and serve only as connecting links between successive notes when such notes are more than a minor second apart.

For example, take the melody of the common chord ascending and descending, as at i. in the following example.

It is allowable to interpolate *passing notes* between these essential notes, which do not affect the bass or harmony. These passing notes are indicated by dots at ii., and are written in the usual way at iii., where the essential notes are distinguished by a horizontal line over them—

It will be observed that in this example the passing notes are placed on the *un*accented parts of the measure. When this is the case they are called "unaccented passing notes."

5. When passing notes occur on the accented part of the measure, they are called "accented passing notes." Example—

These are more dissonant than unaccented passing notes, because they are heard at the same time that the bass and the rest of the harmony are struck, while the unaccented are not heard till afterwards. The following example from Logier will shew this—

It will be remarked that in these examples passing notes are introduced not only into the melody, but also into the bass and inner parts; and that in the three last the inversions of the chord are varied.

6. A chromatic scale may be easily produced by interposing passing notes between the *whole tones* of a diatonic scale; only it is not usual or desirable to insert one between the sixth and seventh degree, as the effect is harsh—

Every one of these inserted semitones might also be harmonized as essential notes, which would involve various modulations. Thus—

NOTE.—When the parts proceed by contrary motion, whole chords may be introduced as "passing chords," intervening between fundamental discords and their resolutions; thus—

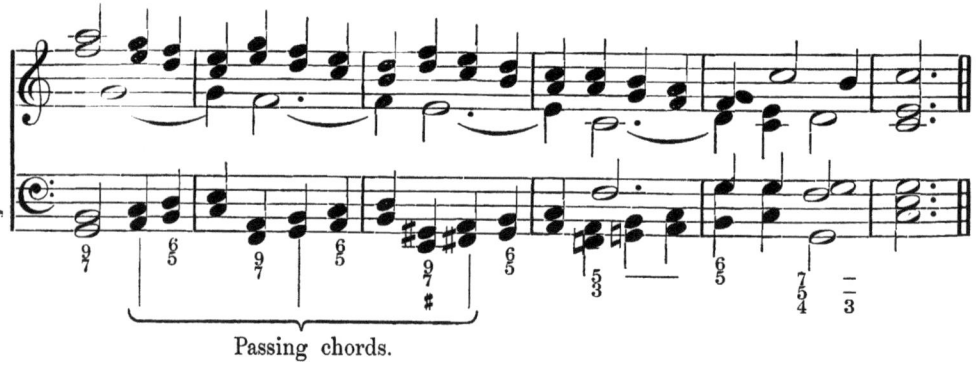

Passing chords.

7. When no passing notes can be introduced, use is made of what are called "*auxiliary notes.*"

They may be written either above or below the melody, and may be either accented or unaccented.

If *below* the melody, they should be only half a tone below.

If *above* the melody, they may be either a half or a whole tone above, as the case requires.

Simple Melody.

Auxiliary Notes added.

Simple Bass.

Auxiliary Notes in the Bass.

8. When the notes of a melody move by a skip, i. e. by intervals greater than a third, passing notes may skip also to a semitone below an ascending interval—

or to a semitone or whole tone above a descending interval—

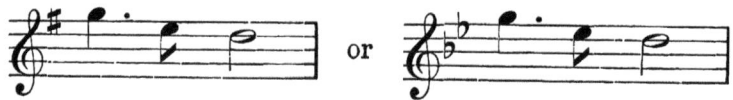 or

Auxiliary notes, under similar circumstances, skip beyond the interval to return—

9. Chromatic passing notes and auxiliary notes, if accented, exercise a very great influence on the harmony; so great, indeed, that it is often difficult to determine whether they should be treated as such, or as real and essential notes—

In this example the A♯ in the second bar is treated here as a chromatic passing note leading from A♮ to B. But it is more than doubtful whether this is not wrong (although it is the usual way of writing it), for the other notes of the chord indicate a change of root, and if the note be written B♭ instead of A♯, it at once shews itself as part of the chord of the minor ninth on root A, superposed on the tonic pedal G, of which A is the supertonic. On the whole it appears therefore preferable to consider this note as an essential one, and to write it B flat, in spite of custom.

In the third bar, on the other hand, the F sharp *must* be treated as an auxiliary note, as it forms no essential part of the harmony of the root A, from which root the chord is evidently derived.

NOTE.—Accented auxiliary notes are usually called "*appoggiaturas*," as they are supposed to be a kind of buttress or leaning support to the note before which they are placed.

10. This last example, in its third bar, introduces another rather doubtful case—

D d 2

For the treble part might be written, with good effect, thus—

in which case the question arises, "What is the derivation of the F sharp?"

It cannot be a passing or auxiliary note, as it moves to D by a skip of a major third.

May it not be an instance of a double-root chord on the roots D and A?

If so, it would be a sort of anticipation of the succeeding chord of D, and would be an analogous case to that remarkable passage in the quartett "When the ear heard her" in Handel's Funeral Anthem—

where the treble goes up to G on the bass A♭, and where the chord is an imperfect "chord of the added sixth" (as it is erroneously called), which we have proved to be derived from the dominant and sub-dominant roots, which here would be $\frac{F}{B\flat}$. This explanation is not altogether conclusive, however, as the major ninth of the F *ought* to be resolved, of course, by descending a whole tone; or, if suspended, it ought to be suspended *in the same part* and *in the same octave*, neither of which conditions is observed in the present case.

It is probably an isolated example of *licence*, peculiar to Handel.

11. In the works of old Church writers of the English school, especially Purcell, Blow, and Croft, it is no uncommon thing to meet with a combination of the minor sixth with the major third, which is treated as a fundamental discord—

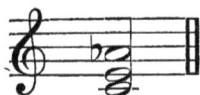

If it *is*, in truth, a fundamental discord, it can be no other than a fundamental minor thirteenth, and of course must be resolved into the key of F.

The thirteenth division in the harmonic series certainly does give a sound which approximates more or less closely to this interval, at least it is not more different from it than the true harmonic fundamental minor seventh is from the tempered minor seventh which we are obliged to use in music; only, whereas the natural minor seventh is *too flat*, the natural minor thirteenth is *too sharp*.

But we may perhaps safely regard the above chord as a fundamental chord of the minor thirteenth, and use it, if need be, with the rest of the harmonic series; thus—

It produces a peculiarly plaintive and pathetic effect when judiciously introduced. But the student should not be too lavish of such extreme discords.

Very often it has more the appearance of an auxiliary note or appoggiatura; for instance—

And at other times it may be looked upon as an ordinary suspension. Of course this can only be when it is regularly prepared in the preceding chord.

There is some difficulty in considering the minor thirteenth as an available portion of the harmonic series of the dominant root, since we have rejected the fundamental eleventh.

But in the first place the harmonic sound which represents the latter interval is nearer to an *augmented* than to a perfect eleventh, whereas the harmonic No. **13** is fairly near to the minor thirteenth.

And in the next place there are really no cases in which the supposed fundamental eleventh may not be equally well regarded either as an inner (or upper) tonic pedal, or as a suspension, or as the minor seventh of the supertonic, as has been already shewn.

It appears therefore unnecessary and unphilosophical to have recourse to the "augmented fourth in the third octave" in the harmonic series, that sound being very much out of tune, more so indeed than any other natural harmonic sound in the first four octaves from the root.

12. Under some circumstances it admits of a doubt whether the chord of the fundamental minor thirteenth may not be more correctly written as an augmented fifth—

for (as has been shewn above, Chapter XI, section 2) nature *does* give us that interval in perfect tune.

And indeed if we invert the minor thirteenth, so as to put it in the bass, it does actually produce a chord of the augmented fifth *—

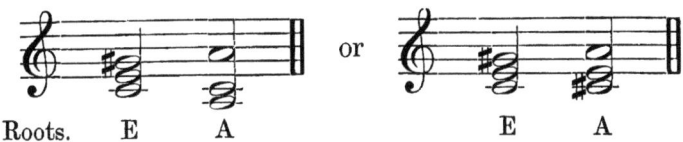

13. The major thirteenth is correct and in tune as found in the series of natural harmonic sounds. It is represented by the cube of 3, or 27. For 3 is the fifth; $3 \times 3 = 9$ is the ninth or supertonic; $3 \times 3 \times 3 = 27$ is a fifth again above that, i. e. the major thirteenth.

* See Short Examples at the end of this book, No. 13.

Hence are probably derived such chords as—

which indeed cannot well be explained in any other consistent way.

14. The province of the science of harmony does not extend further than those various points which have been explained in this treatise.

If the student wishes to become a composer, he must add to these a diligent study of counterpoint, fugue, form, and instrumentation.

Having thus counselled him, we will now leave him to apply what has here been taught, both by analyzing the works of great masters, and by harmonizing melodies according to the rules given in this work.

EXERCISES

ON THE PRECEDING CHAPTERS.

No. 1.—*Exercise on the Chord of the Dominant Seventh.*

(Chapter II, 7, 8.)

Fill in the omitted notes in the incomplete chords.

No. 2.—*Exercise on the Chord of the Added Ninth.*

(Chapter II, 9.)

Fill in the omitted notes in the incomplete chords.

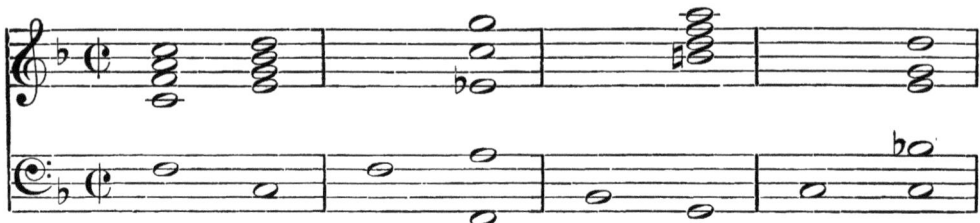

No. 3.—*Exercise on the same.*

Take the two preceding exercises and transpose them into all the major keys.

No. 4.—*Exercise on the Inversions of the Common Chord and their Thorough Bass figuring.*

(Chapter III, 2, 3.)

Fill in the omitted notes according to the figuring.

No. 5.—*Exercise on the Chord of the Dominant Seventh and its Inversions, to be filled in like the last.*

(Chapter III, 3—6.)

No. 6.—*Exercise on the same.*

Transpose the last exercise into all the major keys.

No. 7.—*Exercise on the Inversions of the Chord of the Added Ninth.*
(Chapter III, 9—15.)

No. 8.—*Exercise on the Ascending Major Scale.*

(Chapter IV, 4.)

No. 9.—*Exercise on the Descending Major Scale.*

(Chapter IV, 5, 6.)

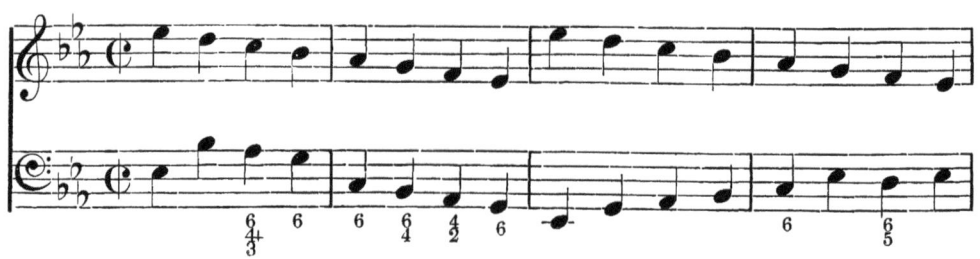

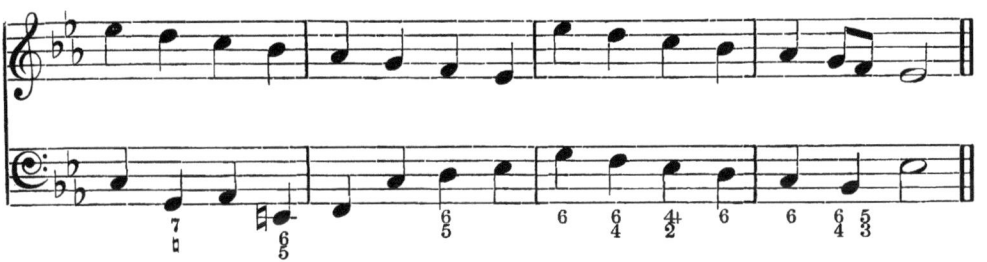

No. 10.—*Exercise on the Ascending Minor Scale.*

(Chapter V, 6.)

No. **11.**—*Exercise on the Chord of the Minor Ninth and its Inversions.*

(Chapter VI, 1—8.)

F f

No. **12.**—*Exercise on the Descending Minor Scale.*

(Chapter VII, 1, 2.)

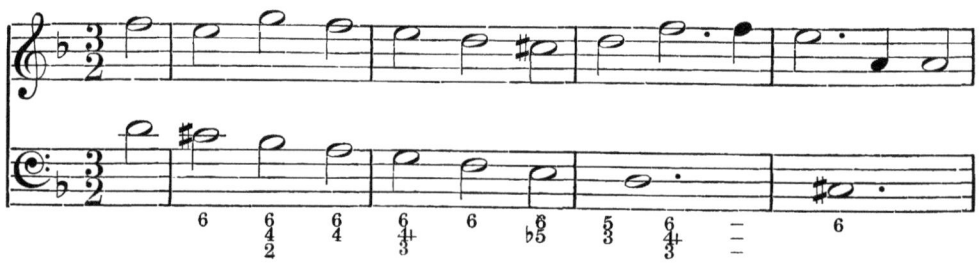

No. 13.—*Exercise on Dissonances by Suspension.*

(Chapter VIII, 3—7.)

No. 14.—*Exercise on Retardations.*

(Chapter IX, 1—4.)

No. 15.—*Exercise on the same.*

No. 16.—*Exercises on the Harmonization of Melodies.*

(Chapter X, 4.)

iii.

No. 17.—*Exercise on the Chord of the Augmented Sixth.*

(Chapter XI, 7, 8.)

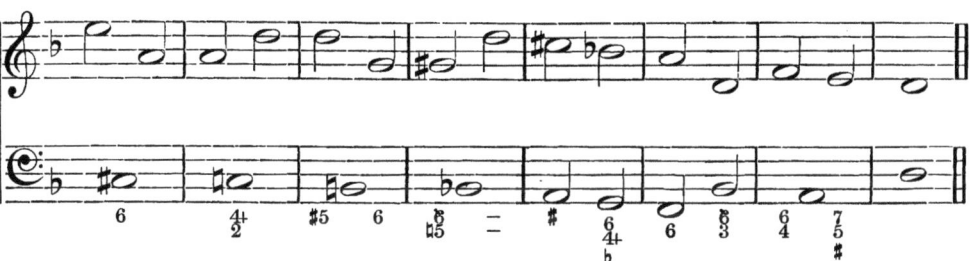

No. 18.—*Exercise on the same with Enharmonic Changes and Inversions.*

(Chapter XI, ♠ 9, 10.)

G g

No. 19.—*Exercise on the Chord of the Minor Seventh and Minor Third and its Inversions.*

(Chapter XII, 3.)

No. 20.—*Exercise on Cadences of all kinds.*

(Chapter XIII, 2—7.)

No. 21.—*Exercise on the same.*

(Chapter XIV, 1.)

G g 2

THE PRINCIPLES OF HARMONY.

No. 22.—*Exercise on Irregular and Deceptive Cadences.*

(Chapter XV, 2—4.)

No. 23.—*Exercise on Modified Basses.*

(Chapter XV, 5—13.)

No. 24.—*Exercise on Sequences.*

(Chapter XVI, 2—6.)

No. 25.—*Exercise on the Introduction of Dominant and Tonic Pedal.*

(Chapter XVII, 1—3.)

Add the two inner parts without figures.

No. 26.—*Exercise on Breaking of Chords.*

(Chapter XVIII, 1.)

Break this harmony in as many ways as possible.

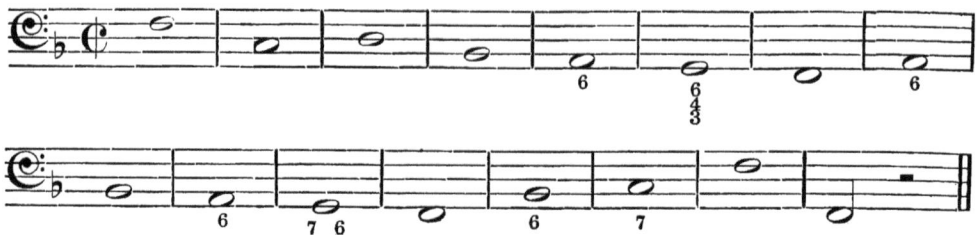

No. 27.—*Exercise on Passing Notes and Auxiliary Notes.*

(Chapter XVIII, 4—8.)

Adorn this melody with passing notes, and with auxiliary notes. The bass and inner parts also.

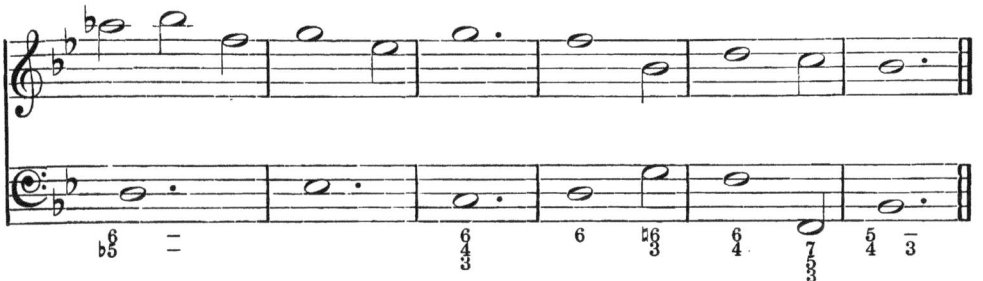

No. 28.—*Exercise on the Chord of the Fundamental Thirteenth and its Inversions.*

H h

List of Fundamental Chords.

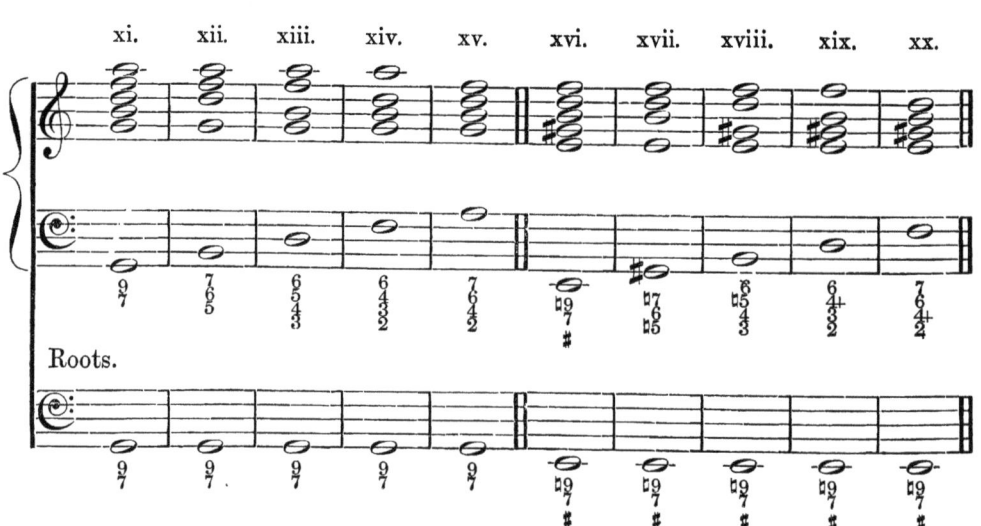

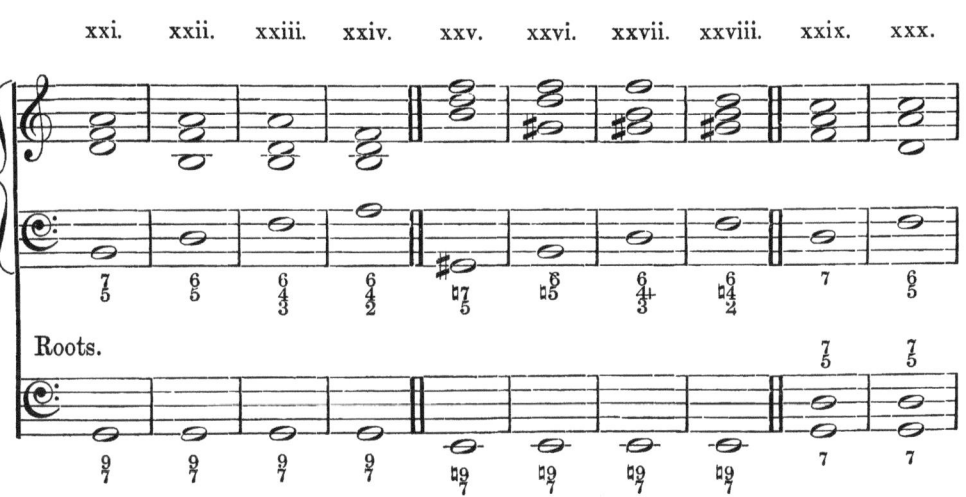

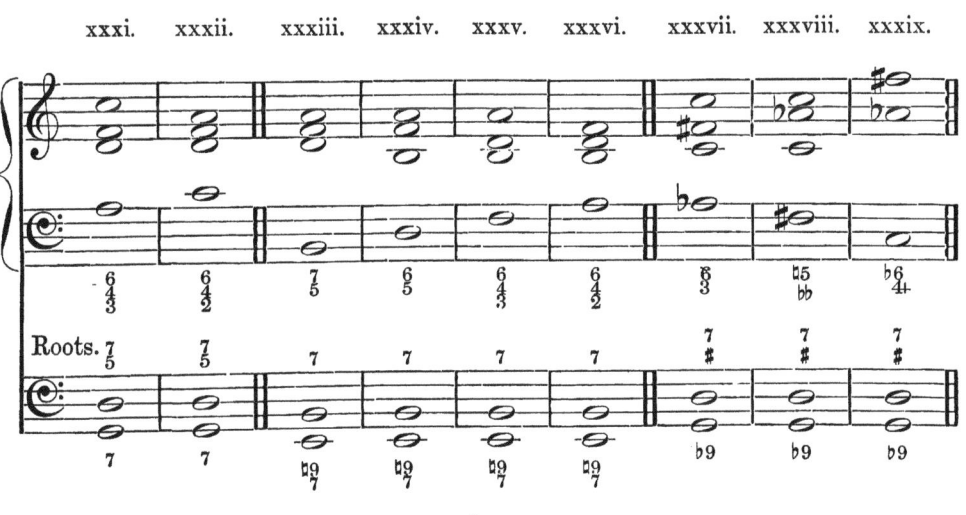

H h 2

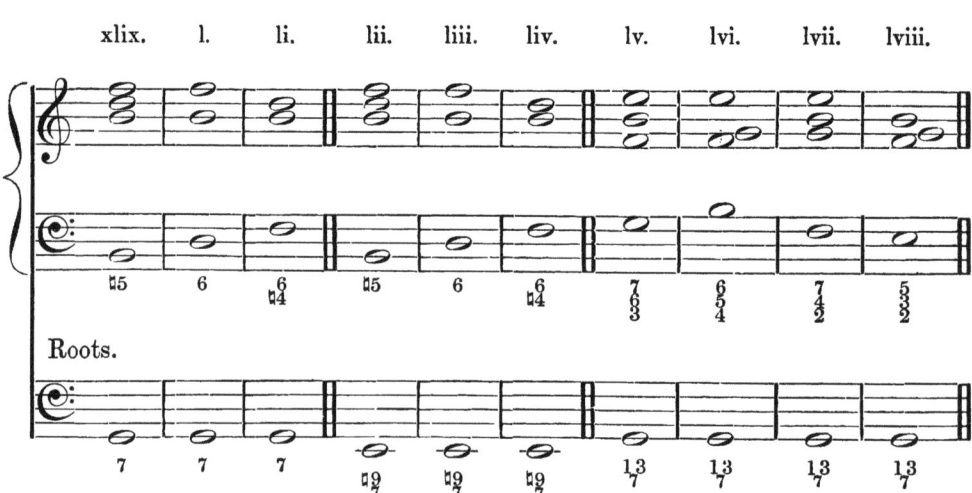

For an explanation of the chords in the above list, the following references are given to the body of the work :—

SHORT EXAMPLES

FROM THE

WORKS OF VARIOUS GREAT MASTERS.

No. 1.

From Weldon's Anthem "Hear my crying," referred to in the note to Chapter XI, section 10.

This is supposed to be the earliest example of an inversion of the chord of the augmented sixth. Here * it is analysed.

No. 2.

et grâ - - - - - - - - - - ce,

Roots.

et grâ - - - - - - - - - ce,

Roots.

From the conclusion of " Robert, toi que j'aime," from Meyerbeer's Opera of " Robert le Diable," where a most pathetic effect is produced by the introduction of the inversion of the chord of the augmented sixth at *, where the D♭ is admirably sustained by the second bassoon.

No. 3.

Som - - bre fo - rêt, de-sert, triste et sau - va - - - ge.

Roots.

From Rossini's Opera "Guillaume Tell." At * the chord of the augmented sixth inverted, and of course based upon a dominant and supertonic root, is introduced on a tonic pedal, thus involving *three* simultaneous roots—*a rare case.*

No. 4.

Roots.

From the opening of Haydn's "Creation," where another inversion of the chord of the augmented sixth is seen at *. This is a very peculiar combination of dominant and supertonic harmonies, as both the roots bear their respective major thirds, and the minor seventh of the supertonic is omitted. The chord marked † is to be regarded as a dissonance by suspension and retardation; but as it is prolonged and emphatic, both the roots are here assigned: for in every case of suspension or retardation two roots must *overlap* of necessity, though it has not been thought requisite always to record them both in the pages of this book. In the following examples it has been thought needless to write the roots in a separate stave.

No. 5.

From a Minuet from Haydn's Symphony in D, where at * we see a chord of the augmented sixth on roots E and B introduced on the pedal A, thus involving *three* simultaneous roots, as in No. 3.

No. 6.

His mighty griefs . . . . re - dress.

From Handel's "Samson." At * there is a very good example of the employment of an enharmonic change, to modulate suddenly from D to E♭.

No. 7.

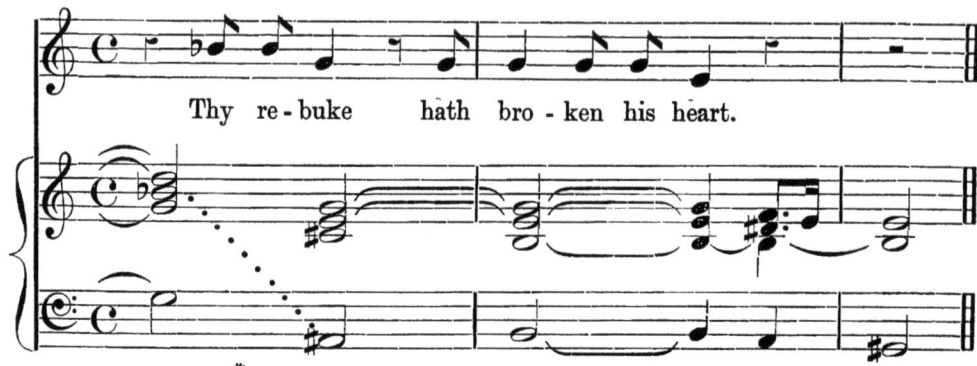

Thy re-buke hath bro-ken his heart.

From Handel's "Messiah." At * there is a beautiful enharmonic change to modulate suddenly from G minor to E minor. Here the enharmonic change is between two different parts of the harmony, instead of the same part, as is usual.

No. 8.

From the chorus "Let Sinai tell," in Crotch's Oratorio "Palestine," where at * there is a chord of the augmented sixth resolved en-harmonically to introduce a sudden modulation from D♯ minor into D♮ major. The effect of this is truly magnificent and sublime.

No. 9.

Example of an inverted dominant pedal from Beethoven's Pastoral Symphony (No. 6).

No. 10.

Example of tonic, dominant, and supertonic pedals combined, from the same. Here, in reality, there is only a *double* pedal, for the supertonic G does not bear any harmony of its own.

No. 11.

From Beethoven's Symphony No. 5, in C minor, where we see a curious and original upper pedal held on by the Clarinet, and singularly resolved by rising chromatically to the leading note of another key, for a transient modulation, in order to introduce the perfect cadence.

No. 12.

My   faith   shall   cling   un - - sha - - - -

- - ken to Thee,   my Sa - - - viour,   to

†   *

Thee, to Thee, my Sa - - - - - viour.

From Spohr's "Crucifixion." At * there is a very clever enharmonic modulation from B♭ minor to E♮ major. At † Spohr has
written E ♮, for convenience of reading, but the note ought to be
written F♭, being the minor ninth of the root E♭.

No. 13.

From the Overture to Mozart's "Zauberflöte." At * the B♮ ought,
theoretically, to be C♭, and it would then be an imperfect inversion
of the chord of the minor thirteenth on the root E♭. As B♮ it could
only form part of the chord of G, which is not possible.

No. 14.

This passage is from De Pearsall's splendid madrigal "Great God of love." At * the seven notes of the diatonic scale are introduced simultaneously, by means of a combination of the chord of the added ninth with all the practicable suspensions and retardations. The effect is admirable.

No. 15.

From the "Cum Sancto Spiritu" in Beethoven's Mass in C. At * there is the fourth inversion of the added ninth irregularly resolved by contrary motion of all the parts.

No. 16.

From Mozart's Quartett in C (No. 6), where in eight bars there are no less than six false relations, in defiance of the general rule. Here they are introduced on purpose, in order to produce a vague, sombre, and mysterious effect—which they do most admirably.

No. 17.

&c.

From Bach's Fugue in C minor (No. 2 of the "Forty-eight Preludes and Fugues"), where there are four false relations in three bars. Here they are merely tolerated for the sake of the "Imitation" in the counterpoint.

No. 18.

From Mendelssohn's "St. Paul." Example of curtailed resolution of the first inversion of the chord of the minor seventh and minor third.

APPENDIX.

EXPLANATION

OF THE

DIAGRAMS OF THE MUSICAL SCALE

AND ITS COMPONENT INTERVALS.

By WILLIAM POLE, F.R.S., Mus. Doc., Oxon.

THE object of these diagrams is to present to the *eye* a representation of the relative magnitudes of the various musical intervals, analogous to the impression which they make upon the *ear*.

The idea of doing this is not new. Mr. Hullah has long adopted the symbol of a ladder representing the diatonic scale, the intervals between the third and fourth, and between the seventh and eighth steps being only one half the length of the other degrees; and I believe somewhat similar figures have been used by other writers; but I am not aware that any attempt has heretofore been made to represent the intervals graphically, with such accuracy as to render appreciable to the eye the minute differences on which the more delicate appreciation of the pitch of the sounds must depend.

I think the diagrams here given will fulfil this condition, as they have been very carefully drawn, and are on a very large scale. The octave is above thirty inches long, giving about two inches and a half for each semitone; and I presume that, on such a scale, the minutest differences of pitch which can be distinguished by a sensitive ear, will be rendered distinct to the eye. For example, the difference between the true fifth, and the fifth of equal temperament, is only about one-fiftieth of a semitone, which few ears could detect except by its beats; yet its existence is made perfectly evident upon the diagram, amounting to a space of about one-twentieth of an inch, or half one of the subdivisions.

A few remarks will explain the principle on which the intervals have been laid down.

The pitch of a note depends on its number of vibrations per second; and it might at first be supposed that by laying down on paper (or, as it is technically termed, "plotting") the vibrations of two given notes by a scale of equal parts, a sufficient representation of the interval between them might be obtained.

But this would not do, for the reason that it would give the same interval different values according to the place in the scale where it was taken, which is at variance with the idea conveyed to the ear.

It is manifest that the idea formed through the ear of the magnitude of any interval— say, for example, of an octave—is the same, whether it be taken at a low pitch, thus—

or at a higher pitch, thus—

But if these were "plotted" on paper by the number of their double vibrations per second, we should have the former represented by

$$132 - 66 = 66 \text{ divisions of the scale,}$$

and the latter by

$$1056 - 528 = 528 \text{ divisions,}$$

which would clearly be inconsistent with the idea sought to be conveyed.

Any representation of spaces derived from the harmonic divisions of the monochord would also fail, for a similar reason.

The more correct method of representation is based on the principle that a musical interval is expressed not by the *difference*, but by the *ratio* of the vibrations of its two sounds; this ratio being always the same, at whatever pitch the interval be taken. We only therefore require a convenient mode of laying down this ratio on paper; and this is obtained, according to a well-known mathematical principle, by the application of logarithms. If two numbers have a definite ratio, the difference between their logarithms will always be equal, whatever the absolute magnitude of the numbers themselves may be. Thus, in the two cases above cited, we have for the example at low pitch

$$\text{log. } 132 \;=\; 2 \cdot 12057$$
$$\text{log. } \;\; 66 \;=\; 1 \cdot 81954$$
$$\text{difference} \quad \cdot 30103$$

For the example at high pitch

$$\text{log. } 1056 \;=\; 3 \cdot 02366$$
$$\text{log. } \;528 \;=\; 2 \cdot 72263$$
$$\text{difference} \quad \cdot 30103$$

To apply this principle, therefore, it is only necessary to take out, from an ordinary table, the logarithms of the numbers of vibrations of any given notes, and the difference of these logarithms will be the *logarithm of their ratio.* And if this latter logarithm be laid down or "plotted" to any convenient scale of equal parts, the interval between the two notes will be thereby represented to the eye, in a manner exactly conformable to the idea conveyed by this interval to the ear.

On this principle the two accompanying diagrams, Plates I and II, have been constructed.

Plate I is a diagram of the extent of an octave, containing all the most usual intermediate intervals. To form this, a scale of inches, subdivided into tenths, having been first drawn on the paper, the logarithmic difference representing the ratio of the octave ($\cdot 30103$), magnified one hundred times, was laid down so as to occupy $30 \cdot 103$ of these divisions, and within this space were also marked the other intervals, calculated in like manner. Thus 17·609 inches, corresponding to the log. of $\frac{3}{2}$, formed the interval of the perfect fifth; and 9·691 inches, corresponding to the log. of $\frac{5}{4}$, formed the major third, and so on.

The centre, or widest column of the figure, gives the diatonic scale; the chromatic notes being placed in narrower columns on each side, the sharps to the left, and the flats to the right.

It will be seen that many of the notes have been given two values; these are the equivocal notes, the exact pitch of which may be deduced in two ways, giving two different values for them. For example, the second of the scale, D, may either be deduced as the fifth above G (= 5·115), or as the fourth below A (= 4·576), the former making it a major tone above the tonic, the latter a minor tone. Similarly the minor seventh B♭ may be deduced either as a minor third above G (= 25·527), or as a perfect fourth above F (= 24·988), and so on for others.

On each side of the true scale is placed a column giving the positions of the various notes as determined by the system of equal temperament, each semitone interval being equal, and = 2·5086 inches of the logarithmic scale. The nature of the errors induced by this mode of temperament will be obvious by simple inspection.

To the right of the before-mentioned scales are five columns, designed to shew the natural harmonic notes to the fundamental tonic, up to the thirty-second, which is probably higher than they can ever be actually distinguished in practice, even with artificial aids. They are laid down by the logarithmic values of their intervals from the fundamental, in the same way as the notes of the scale, except that in the second, third, fourth, and fifth columns the equivalents for one, two, three, and four octaves respectively, are subtracted from those of the true intervals, in order to bring the whole of the notes within the compass of one octave. This will be clearly explained by Tables **B** and **C**.

The names of the notes marked on the diagram are arranged for the scale of C, i. e. C being the fundamental or tonic, this being the simplest scale to select for an example; but the same arrangement of lines would answer for any other fundamental by merely changing the names attached.

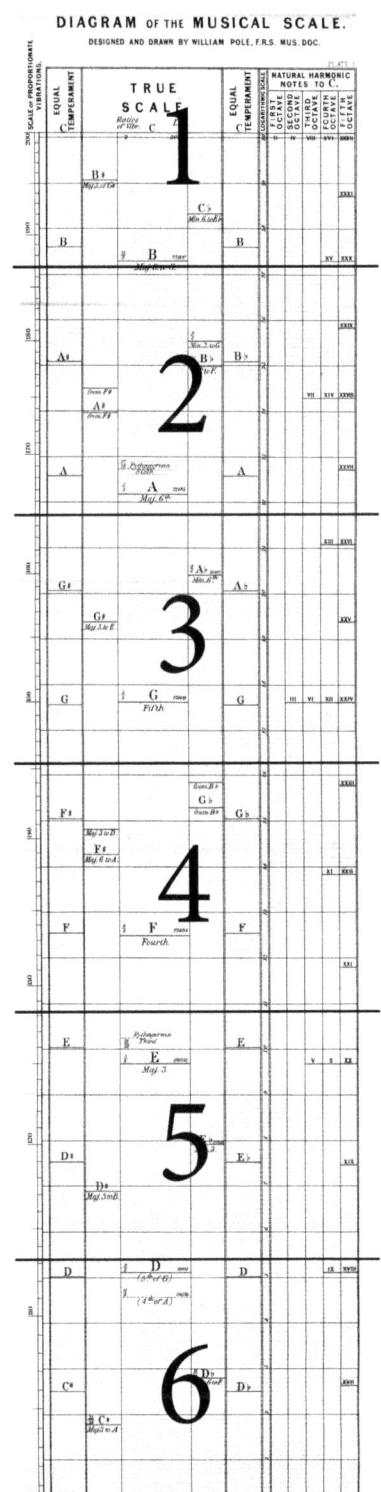

Key to following pages.

DIAGRAM OF THE MUSICAL SCALE.

DESIGNED AND DRAWN BY WILLIAM POLE, F.R.S. MUS. DOC.

PLATE 1

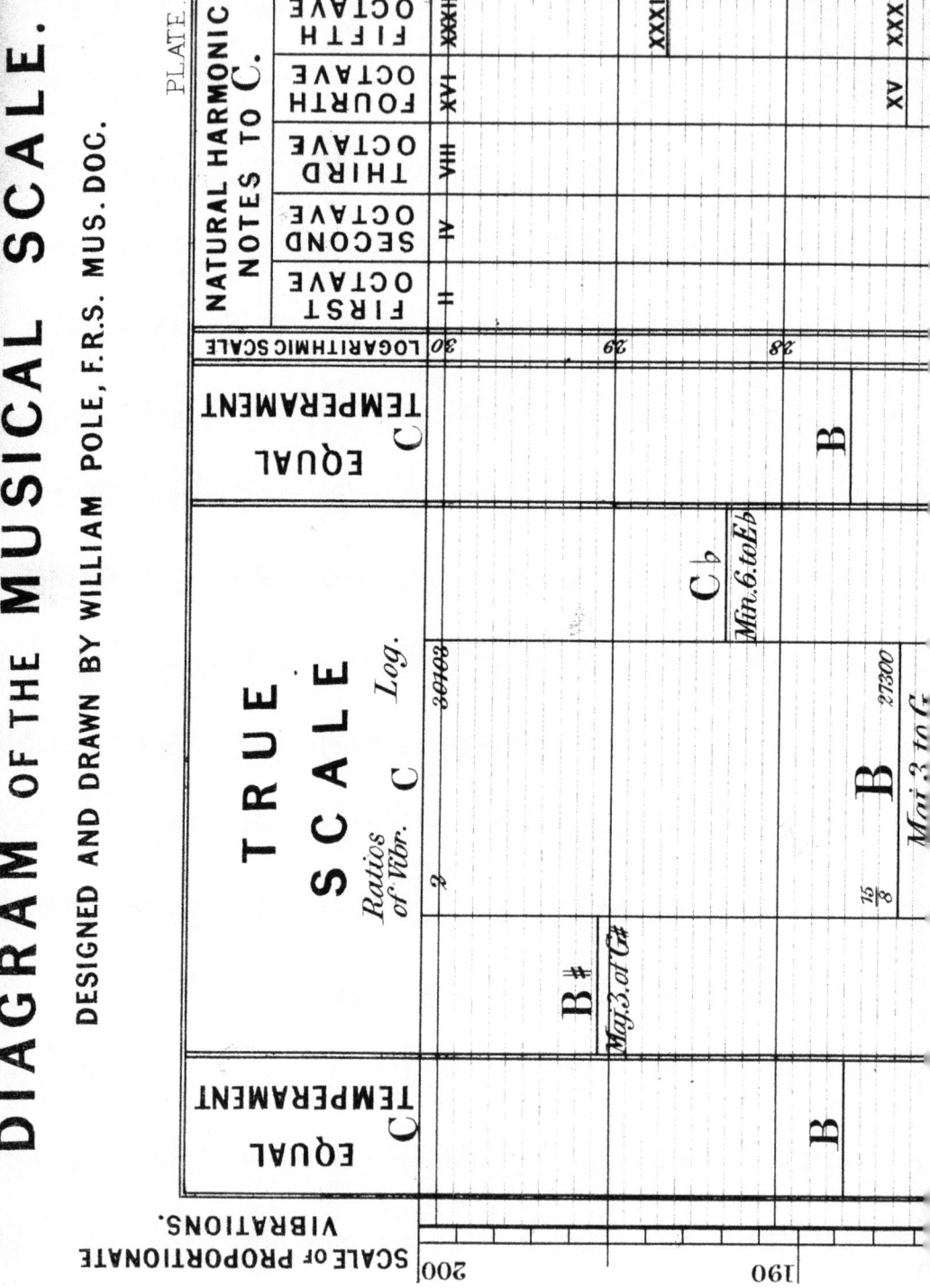

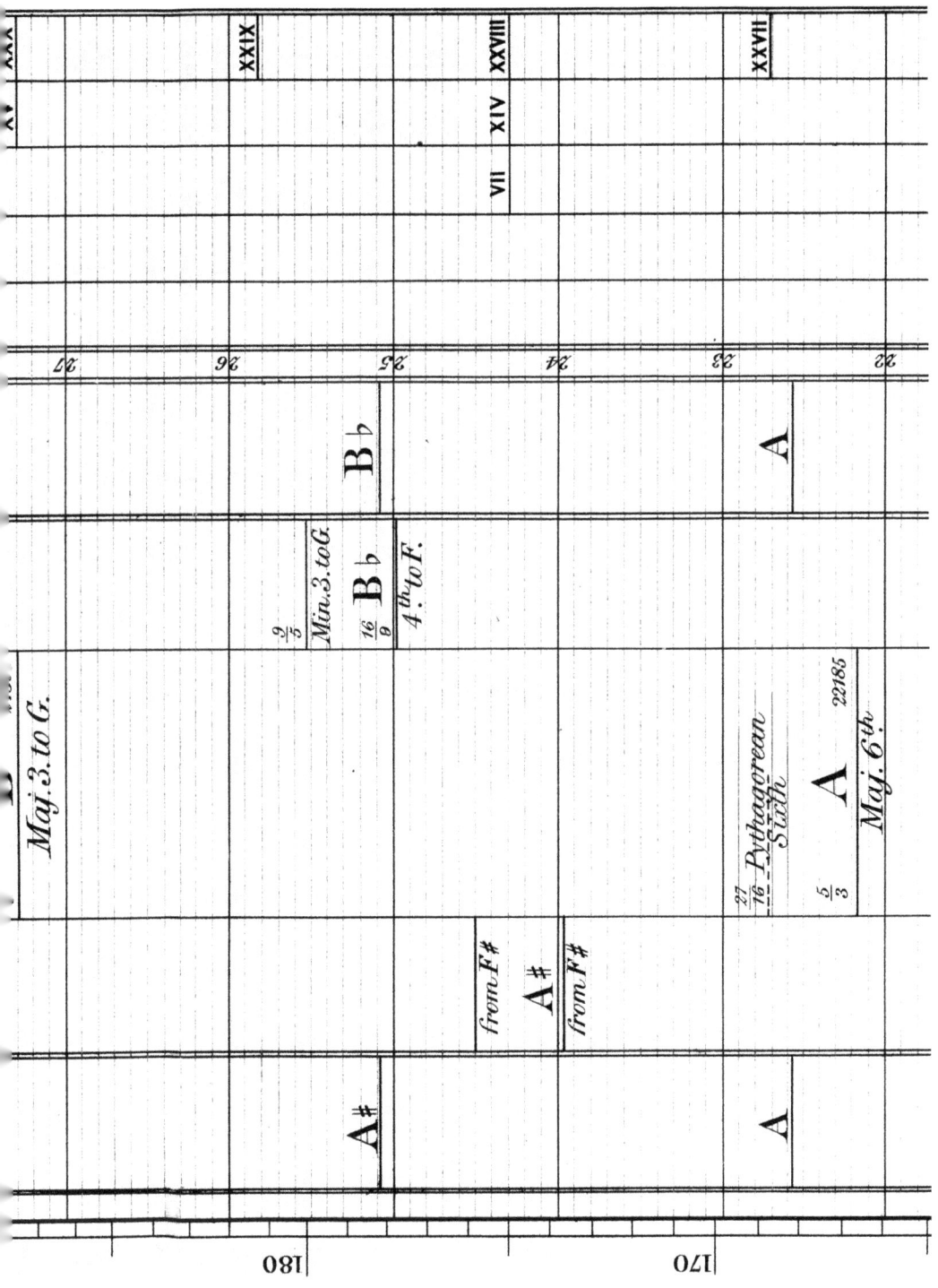

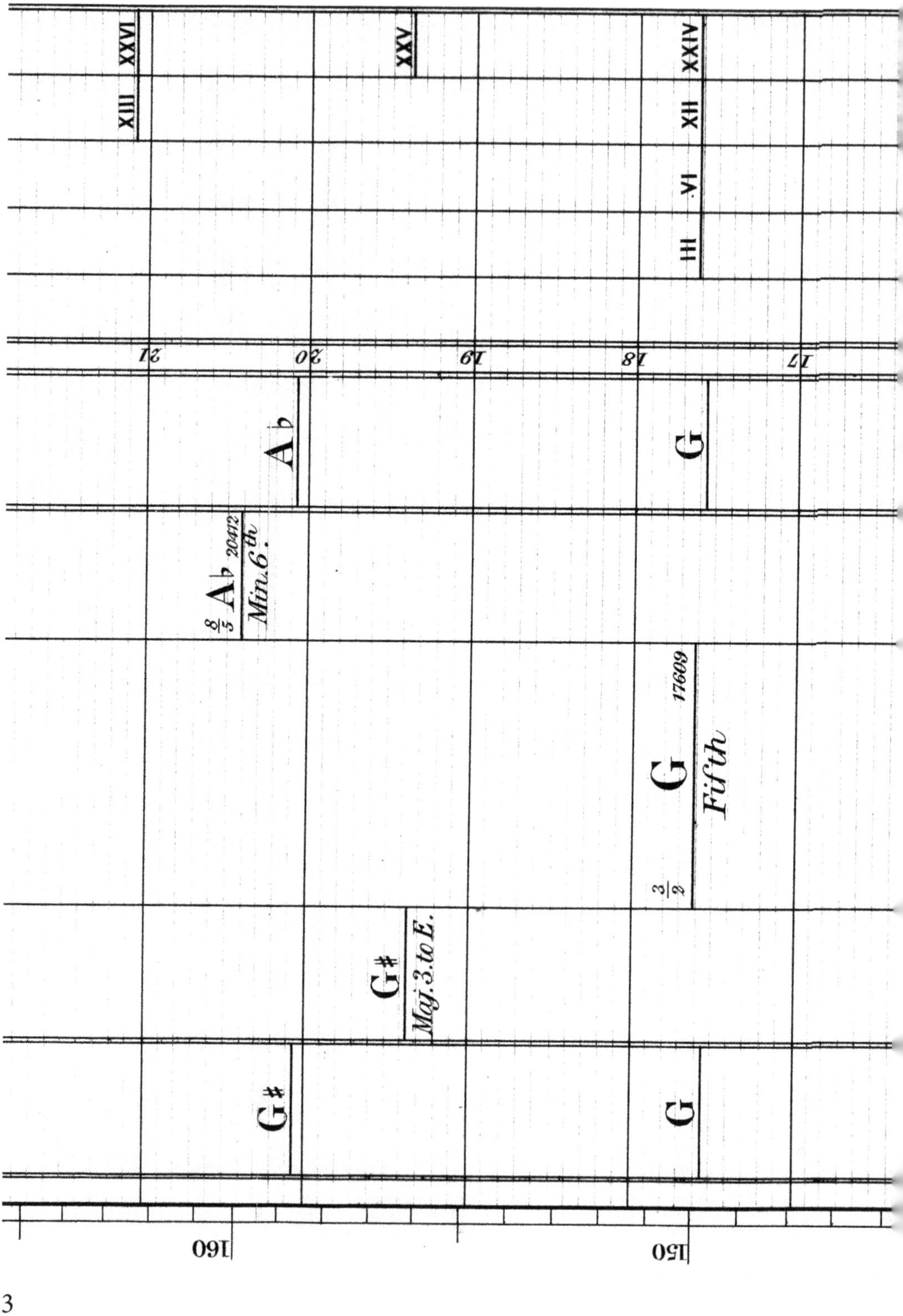

XXVI XXV XXIV

XIII XII VI III

21 20 19 18 17

A♭

G

$\frac{8}{5}$ A♭ 20412 Min.6th.

G 17609 Fifth $\frac{3}{2}$

G♯ Maj.3.to E.

G♯

G

160

150

3

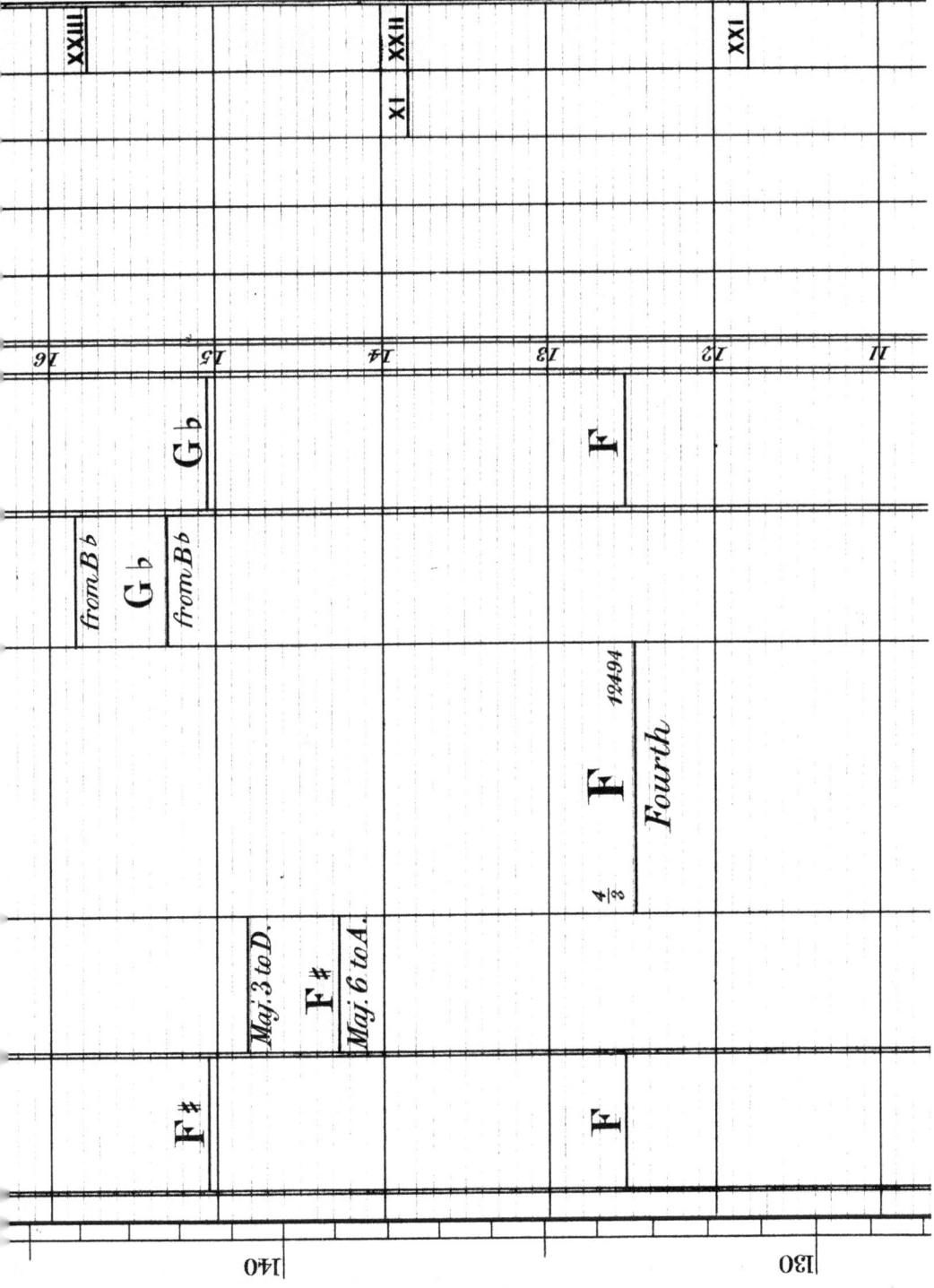

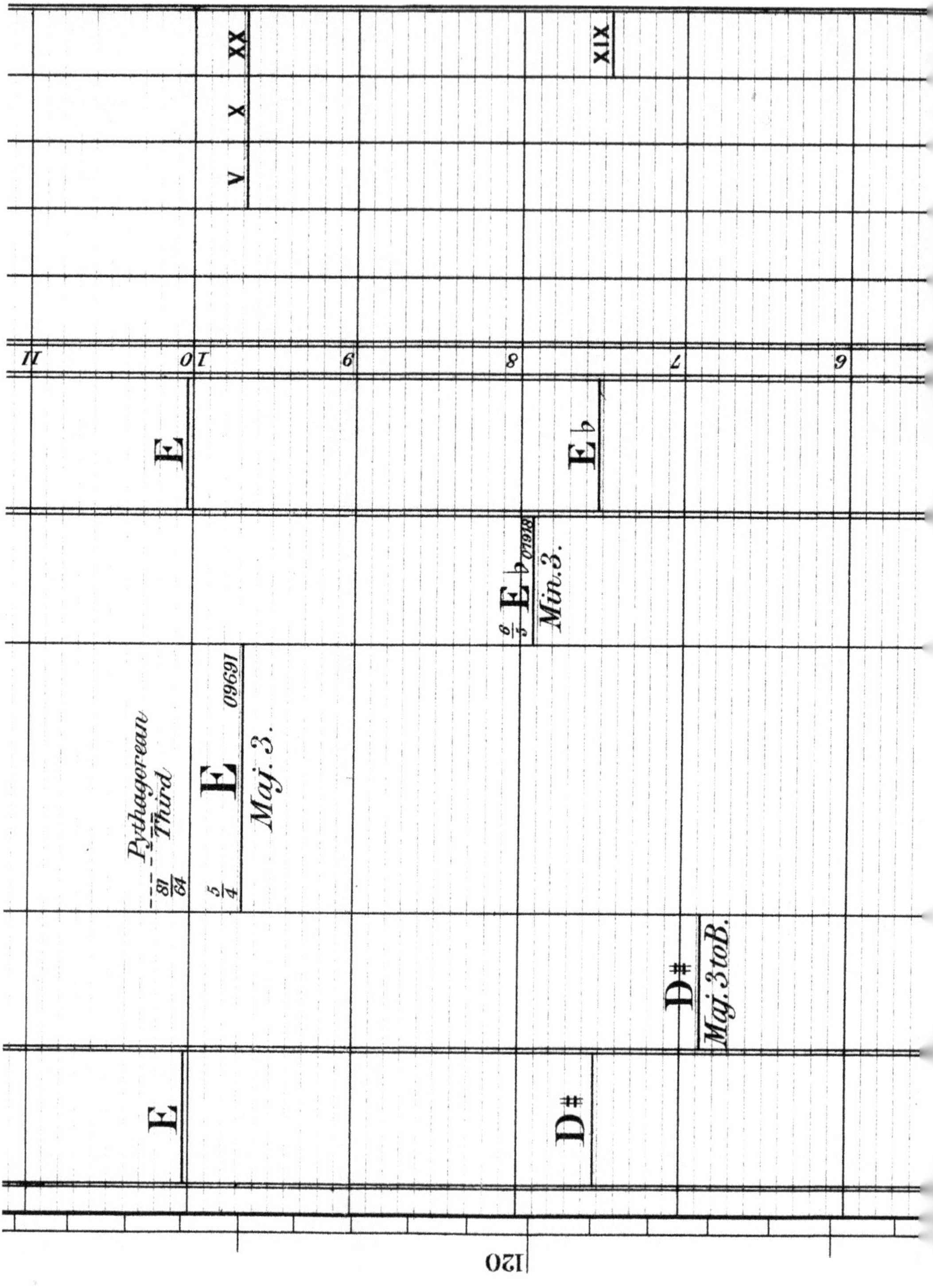

XX

XIX

X

V

II

10

9

8

7

6

E

E♭

6/5 E♭ 3986.0
Min.3.

Pythagorean Third
81/64

5/4 E 1696.0
Maj.3.

E

D#
Maj.3 to B.

D#

120

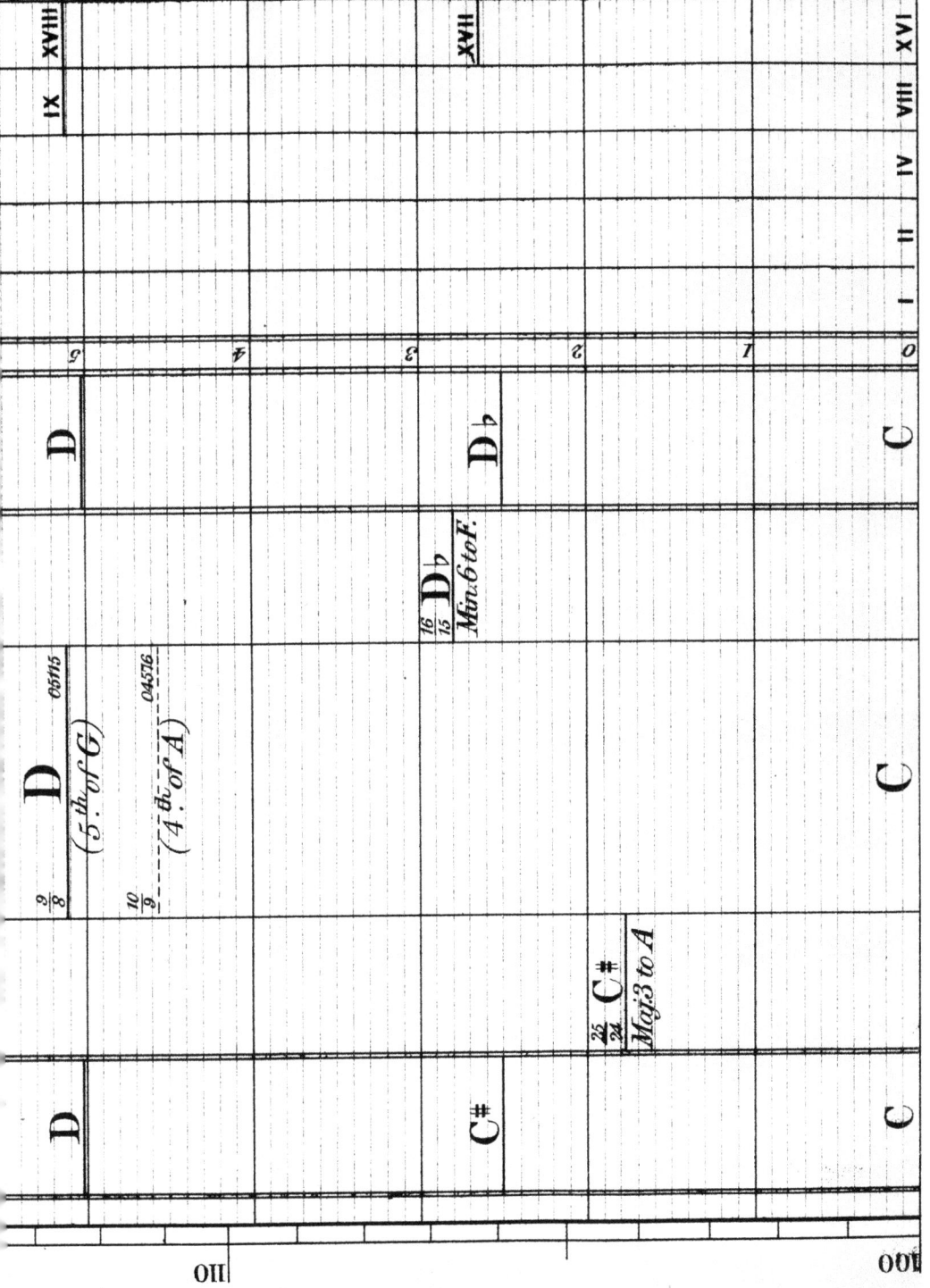

DIAGRAM OF VARIOUS SMALL INTERVALS.

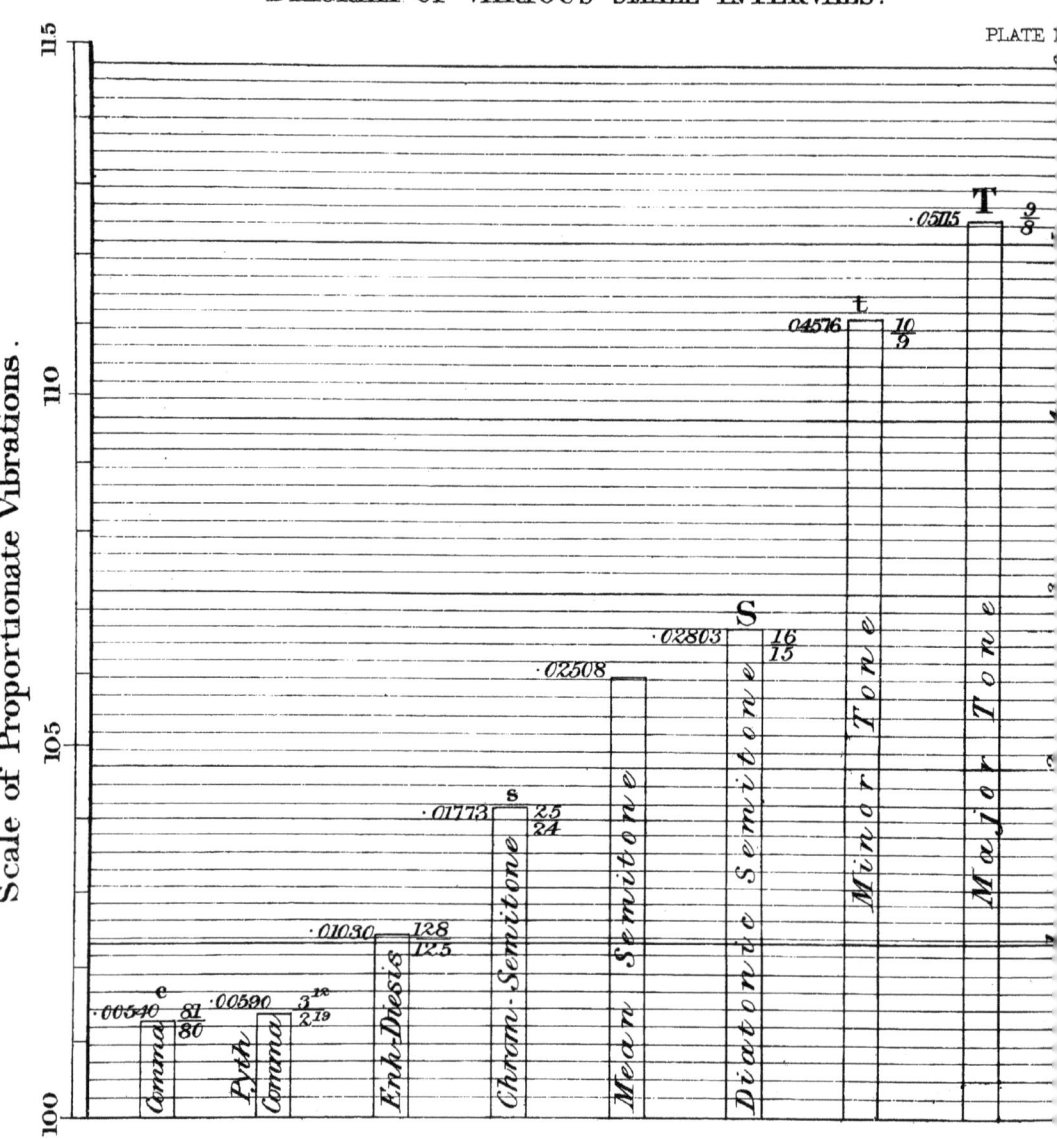

Scale of Proportionate Vibrations.

On the left of the diagram is a " Scale of Proportionate Vibrations," which shews the number of vibrations made by any of the notes marked, in proportion to those of the fundamental, the latter being taken as 100. This is in fact the scale of natural numbers, to which the divisions of the diagram are the logarithms.

The smaller diagram, Plate II, contains representations of several small intervals, drawn on the same principle and to the same scale as those in the larger diagram.

The Table **A** gives a list of the various intervals (except the harmonics) contained in Diagrams I and II, with full particulars respecting their derivation and composition, their exact ratios, and the logarithmic numbers by which their places in the diagrams have been determined.

Tables **B** and **C** are devoted to the harmonics only, as already explained.

The intervals on the diagram may be measured and compared either with a pair of compasses, or by marking the distances down on a strip of paper.

LONDON,
March, 1868.

A.

TABLE OF THE VARIOUS MUSICAL INTERVALS CONTAINED IN DIAGRAMS I AND II.

The number in the last column determines the magnitude of the interval as laid down in the diagram.

Limiting Notes.	Name of the Interval.	Derivation of the Higher Note.	Composition of the Interval (logarithmic)	Ratio of Vibrations of the two Limiting Sounds.	Logan of t Rat
C—C	Octave	. . . . . .	. . . .	2 : 1	·301
C—B$\sharp$	. . . . . .	Major third above G$\sharp$	Three major thirds	125 : 64	·290
C—C$\flat$	Diminished octave	Minor sixth above E$\flat$	{ Minor third + minor sixth; or octave − s . . . . }	48 : 25	·283
C—B	Major seventh . .	Equal temperament . / True interval . . .	Eleven mean semitones . . . / Fifth + major third	. . . / 15 : 8	·275 / ·273
C—B$\flat$	Minor seventh . .	Minor third above G . / By equal temperament / Fourth above F . . .	Fifth + minor third . . . . . / Ten mean semitones . . . . / Two perfect fourths	9 : 5 / . . . / 16 : 9	.255 / ·250 / ·249
C—A$\sharp$	Augmented sixth .	Major third above F$\sharp$. / do. do. . . .	Major seventh − S . . . . . / Major sixth + s	225 :128 / 125 : 72	·244 / ·239
C—A	Major sixth . . .	Pythagorean . . . . / By equal temperament / True	Three fifths − one octave . . . / Nine mean semitones . . . . / { Minor sixth + s; or fifth + t; or fourth + major third . . . }	27 : 16 / . . . / 5 : 3	·227 / ·225 / ·221
C—A$\flat$	Minor sixth . . .	True . . . . . . / By equal temperament	Fifth + S; or fourth + minor third / Eight mean semitones . . .	8 : 5 / . . .	·204 / ·200
C—G$\sharp$	Augmented fifth .	Major third to E . .	Two major thirds	25 : 16	·193
C—G	Perfect fifth . .	True . . . . . . / By equal temperament	. . . . / Seven mean semitones . . .	3 : 2 / . . .	·176 / ·175
C—G$\flat$	Diminished fifth .	Major third below B$\flat$. / do. do. . . . / By equal temperament	Fifth − s . . . . / Fourth + S . . . . / Six mean semitones	36 : 25 / 64 : 45 / . . .	·158 / ·152 / ·150

ting es.	Name of the Interval.	Derivation of the Higher Note.	Composition of the Interval (logarithmic).	Ratio of Vibrations of the two Limiting Sounds	Logarithm of this Ratio.
F♯	Tritone or augmented fourth . . .	Major third above D .	Fifth − S; or $T + T + t$ . . .	45 : 32	·14806
		Minor third below A .	Fourth + s; or $T + t + t$ . . .	25 : 18	·14267
F	Perfect fourth . .	By equal temperament	Five mean semitones	. . .	·12543
		True	Major third + S	4 : 3	·12494
E	Major third . . .	Pythagorean , . . .	Four fifths − two octaves . .	81 : 64	·10230
		By equal temperament	Four mean semitones	. . .	·10034
		True . . . . .,	$T + t$; or minor third + s . .	5 : 4	·09691
E♭	Minor third . . .	True . , ...	$T + S$	6 : 5	·07918
		By equal temperament	Three mean semitones . . .	. . .	·07526
D♯	Augmented second	Minor sixth below B .	Major seventh − minor sixth; or $T + s$	75 : 64	·06888
D	Major second . .	Fifth above G . . .	Tone major $(T) = t + c$ . . .	9 : 8	·05115
		By equal temperament	Two mean semitones	. . .	·05017
		Fifth below A . . .	Tone minor $(t) = S + s$	10 : 9	·04576
D♭	Minor second . .	Major third below F .	Diatonic semitone (S)	16 : 15	·02803
		By equal temperament	One mean semitone	. . .	·02509
C♯	Augmented unison	Minor sixth below A .	Chromatic semitone (s) . . .	25 : 24	·01773
-D♭)	Enharmonic Diesis	. . . .	$S − s$	128 : 125	·01030
	Pythagorean comma	. . . .	Twelve fifths − seven octaves .	3^{12} : 2^{19}	·00590
	Ordinary comma (c)	. . . .	$T − t$	81 : 80	·00540
C	Unison	. . . .	. . . .	1 : 1	·00000

M m

B.

TABLE OF THE NATURAL HARMONIC NOTES TO C.

The sign + signifies that the harmonic note is sharper than the one named, the sign — flatter.

Number in rank.	Upper note, the lower one being C C C.	Octave.	Ratio of Vibrations.	Logarithm of this ratio.
1	C C C	First Octave	1 : 1	·00000
2	C C		2 : 1	·30103
3	G G	Second Octave	3 : 1	·47712
4	C		4 : 1	·60206
5	E		5 : 1	·69897
6	G	Third Octave	6 : 1	·77815
7	B♭ —		7 : 1	·84510
8	c		8 : 1	·90309
9	d		9 : 1	·95424
10	e		10 : 1	1·00000
11	f♯ —		11 : 1	1·04139
12	g	Fourth Octave	12 : 1	1·07918
13	a♭ +		13 : 1	1·11394
14	b♭ —		14 : 1	1·14613
15	b		15 : 1	1·17609
16	c̄		16 : 1	1·20412
17	d̄♭ —		17 : 1	1·23045
18	d̄		18 : 1	1·25527
19	ē♭		19 : 1	1·27875
20	ē		20 : 1	1·30103
21	f̄ —		21 : 1	1·32222
22	f̄♯ —		22 : 1	1·34242
23	ḡ♭		23 : 1	1·36173
24	ḡ	Fifth Octave	24 : 1	1·38021
25	ḡ♯		25 : 1	1·39794
26	ā♭ +		26 : 1	1·41497
27	ā		27 : 1	1·43136
28	b̄♭ —		28 : 1	1·44716
29	b̄♭ +		29 : 1	1·46240
30	b̄		30 : 1	1·47712
31	c̄♭ +		31 : 1	1·49136
32	c̄		32 : 1	1·50515

C.

TABLE OF HARMONIC NOTES TO C, COMPRESSED INTO ONE OCTAVE.

The number in the last column determines the position of the note in the diagram.

Number in rank.	Upper note, the lower one being C.	Ratio of Vibrations.	Logarithm of this ratio.
2, 4, 8, 16, 32	C	2 : 1	·30103
31	C♭ +	31 : 16	·28724
15, 30	B	15 : 8	·27300
29	B♭ +	29 : 16	·25828
7, 14, 28	B♭ −	7 : 4	·24304
27	A	27 : 16	·22724
13, 26	A♭ +	13 : 8	·21085
25	G♯	25 : 16	·19382
3, 6, 12, 24	G	3 : 2	·17609
23	G♭	23 : 16	·15761
11, 22	F♯ −	11 : 8	·13830
21	F −	21 : 16	·11810
5, 10, 20	E	5 : 4	·09691
19	E♭	19 : 16	·07463
9, 18	D	9 : 8	·05115
17	D♭	17 : 16	·02633
2, 4, 8, 16	C	1 : 1	·00000

For EU product safety concerns, contact us at Calle de José Abascal, 56–1°, 28003 Madrid, Spain or eugpsr@cambridge.org.

www.ingramcontent.com/pod-product-compliance
Ingram Content Group UK Ltd.
Pitfield, Milton Keynes, MK11 3LW, UK
UKHW020456240426
470322UK00016B/384

* 9 7 8 1 1 0 8 0 3 0 2 2 9 *